Marriage Bonds
and
Ministers' Returns
of
Charlotte County
Virginia
- 1764-1815 -

Compiled By:
Catherine Lindsay Knorr

Southern Historical Press, Inc.
Greenville, South Carolina

SOUTHERN HISTORICAL PRESS, INC.
PO BOX 1267
Greenville, SC   29601

ISBN #0-89308-262-7

Printed in the United States of America

To
My two sweet daughters-in-law
Myra Bell Bridges Greer
(Mrs. Willis Roswell Greer)
and
Lois Wright Hatcher Greer
(Mrs. Hal Wyche Greer, II)
who keeps my sons perfectly happy,
thereby reaping my eternal
gratitude and love.

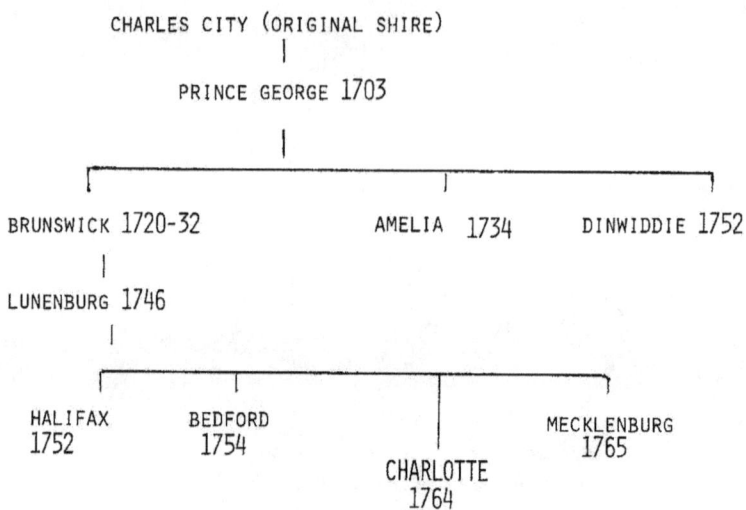

CHARLES CITY (ORIGINAL SHIRE)

PRINCE GEORGE 1703

BRUNSWICK 1720-32   AMELIA 1734   DINWIDDIE 1752

LUNENBURG 1746

HALIFAX   BEDFORD   MECKLENBURG
1752   1754   1765
                          CHARLOTTE
                          1764

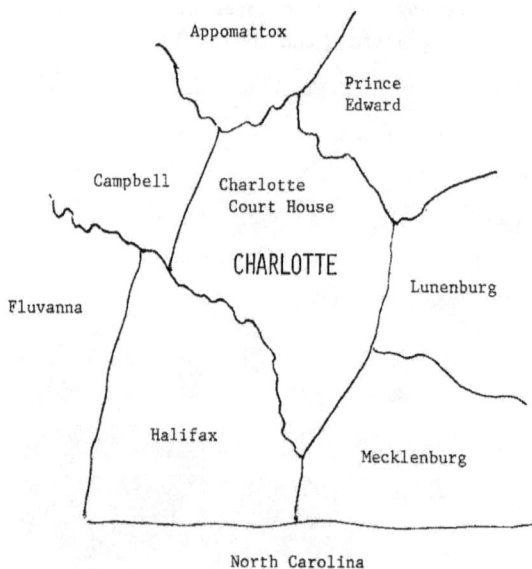

Appomattox

Prince
Edward

Campbell   Charlotte
                  Court House

                  CHARLOTTE

Fluvanna   Lunenburg

          Halifax

                          Mecklenburg

          North Carolina

Publisher's Preface

Mrs. Knorr died in 1975, and after her death these books of marriage records were kept in print and sold by her late husband. Upon his death, they became the property of her grandson, Hal Wyche Greer, III, of Marietta, Georgia, who continued to sell them on a limited basis.

In mid-1981 I sought to find Mr. Greer to discuss with him the possibility of obtaining the exclusive publishing and sales rights to these 14 titles. In due time, Mr. Greer and I were able to negotiate a contract for my exclusive sales and publication rights to these books. It was agreed that Mr. Greer would have a final voice on the changing of the format of any of these titles when they needed to be reprinted. I suggested to Mr. Greer that when these various books sold out and a reprinting had to be done, that for the sake of cost, I would publish them in a 6" x 9" page size, but that the format and style would remain the same, and this was agreed upon.

The reader is cautioned to note that these new 6 x 9 pages are typed verbatum from Mrs. Knorr's original copy, and page by page, so that new indexing was not required. It was also decided that when a book went out of print, it would be retyped on an electric typewriter with a carbon ribbon for better legibility. As publisher, I felt it was important to call to the attention of the reader these changes and the reason for eventually bringing out all of these titles in a 6 x 9 book.

The Rev. S. Emmett Lucas, Jr.
Publisher

Preface

When I asked Dr. Joseph D. Eggleston, in April 1950, which County I should do next, his emphatic reply way, "Charlotte, by all means. It is an untouched county."

So, April 1951 found me in Charlotte Court House, copying marriages. And I am glad, because now I know where I am going when I retire. Straight to Charlotte.

To Charlotte where purple finches by the dozen frolic in the grass, (I had never before seen more than one at a time); where country-cousin dandelions and city-cousin violets grow together all along the road side; where there are unbelievable cascades of molten gold (forsythia, to you) and mammoth bouquets of rose, (could be peach trees); great corsages of frosty pink which will, no doubt, have crab apples come summer.

Charlotte, where no trains or busses run and where the grocery store of red brick has, so help me, four tall white columns supporting a classic Greek pediment. Where no whistles blow and there is no town clock to strike. But where there is plenty of peace and quiet, friend-liness and charm.

This is where Patrick Henry lived and died and lies buried at "Red Hill". This is where John Randolph lived and died at "Roanoke": where these two brilliant men had their famous debate on States Rights on that March day so long ago in 1799.

In 1781 when General Green retreated through North Carolina, pursued by Cornwallis, crossed the Dan River, halted and called for reinforcements, the Charlotte Militia turned out en masse.

The names of the officers of Charlotte Militia are worthy of last-ing remembrance. They were: Col. Thomas Read, Lt. Col. Joel Watkins, Lt. Col. Josiah Morton: Captains William Morton, James Morton, Gideon Spencer, Richard Gaines, Jr., William Jameson, White, Barksdale, Holloway and Wallace. Other distinguished officers included Col. Clement Carrington.

Six companies of Charlotte infantry were in Pickett's Division that make the celebrated charge at Gettysburg, which, for sheer bravery has no equal in history.

Charlotte County, formed in 1764 from Lunenburg (Hening VIII 41 and Journal of the House of Burgesses 27 November 1764) was named for the young queen of George III, the Princesses Charlotte Sophia of Mecklenberg. (Long's Virginia County Names p 54: Robinson p 47). The first clerk was Samuel Cobbs and the first sheriff Thomas Read, they having taken the oath 1 December 1764. Both gentlemen held their commissions from the Honorable Thomas Nelson, Secretary of the Colony.

The first Court was held 4 March 1765, with the following Gentlemen Justices present: James Hunt, David Caldwell, Thomas Spencer, Thomas Bedford, Elisha White, Joseph Morton and John White.

The first act of the Court was to "set and state the prices of Liquors, Diet, Lodging and Provinder". West Indian Rum was 10 shillings a gallon, New England rum only 6. Good Virginia "cyder" 4 pence a quart, apple brandy 6 shillings a gallon, breakfast 8 pence, oats 4 pence a gallon, lodging "with clean sheets" 6 pence.

The first members of the House of Burgesses from Charlotte were Paul Carrington and Clement Read (Stanard's Colornial Virginia Register p 171). Probably no man gave more years of his life to the service of County and State than did Paul Carrington. For forty-two years he held public trust, twenty-nine of them in the judiciary department.

I could go on and on, but this is supposed to be a book of the marriage bonds and ministers' returns of Charlotte County.

Turn just one more page!

Mrs. H. A. Knorr
1401 Linden Street
Pine Bluff, Arkansas

Caution!

Please look for all spellings of a name viz.: Hamblett - Hamlett; Hoard - Hord; Stoe - Stowe; Hailey - Haley; Childress - Childray; Gankins - Ginkins; Wilmouth - Wilmutt - Wilmot; Laine - Lane; Fowlks - Fulks; Brooke - Brooks. Biggs and Diggs got themselved mixed up, as did Reverley and Beverley. Such variations in spelling keep a genealogist on the alert to note and cross index different interpretations of what is obviously the same name.

No liberties with spelling have been taken except in the instance of nicknames. Where Suckey was given on the bond and Susanna appears in the ministers' returns I have used the correct name, Susanna. So with Anne and Nancy; Martha and Patsey.

Most of the discrepancies between the bonds and ministers' returns are in the dates. But when we realize the ministers often made their returns in the County Court from memory and months after the wedding, it is surprising that they are as accurate as we find them.

There is a tragic break in Charlotte County Marriage Bonds between 1815 and 1850. Although it made this volume larger than any of my others, I have given you all of the bonds up to and including 1815, and of course the ministers' returns to the same period.

C. L. K.

20 September 1787. David ADAMS and Mary Johnson, dau. Reuben Johnson. Sur. James Adams. Married by Rev. John Williams. p 100

12 June 1772. James ADAMS and Jenny Cunningham, dau. James Cunningham. James son of John Adams. Sur. Samuel Cunningham. p 13

3 June 1782. James ADAMS and Leanna Sullivant (widow). Sur. William Morton. p 51

23 May 1787. James ADAMS and Mary Stowe, dau. Joel Stowe. Sur. William Stowe. Married 26 May by Rev. John Weatherford. p 101

16 October 1788. James ADAMS, Jr. and Mary Prusit, dau. Joseph Prusit. Sur. David Adams. Married same day by Rev. John Williams who says Mary Prewit. p 111

22 October 1813. James ADAMS and Mary Bouldin, dau. Richard Bouldin. Sur. Thomas T. Bouldin. p 497

10 December 1812. John A. ADAMS and Polly Cook, dau. Thomas Cook. Sur. James Brown. John A. son of Leannah Adams. Married 17 December by Rev. John Chappell. p 482

20 October 1786. Thomas ADAMS and Sally Ford, dau. Culverain Ford. Sur. Abner Barksdale. Married by Rev. Thomas Johnston who says October 4. p 94

1 August 1785. William ADAMS and Keturah Ford. Sur. Culverine Ford. Married 4 August by Rev. Thomas Johnston. p 80

22 February 1790. William ADAMS and Susannah Maddox. Sur. James Adams. Married 25 February by Rev. John Weatherford. p 141

3 February 1794. William ADAMS and Sally Brown. Sur. Burwell Brown. Married 6 February by Rev. Edward Almond. p 208

17 April 1797. Henry ADKERSON and Anne Lee (widow). Sur. Charles Newcomb. p 260

2 August 1790. William ADKINS and Sally Ryon. Sur. William Ryon. p 140

7 January 1793. Peter AKERS and Matsey Harroway, dau. Charles Harroway who is surety. Returned to May 1793 Court by Rev. John Chappell. p 197

27 January 1803. James ALDERSON and Nancy Stokes. Sur. Samuel Green. James son of Mary Alderson. Married 28 January by Rev. Edward Almond. p 335

7 December 1778. John ALDERSON and Keziah Foster, dau. Thomas Foster who is surety. p 29

14 July 1807. Archibald A. ALEXANDER and Fannie Morton, ward of William L. Morton who is surety. p 400

12 November 1767. Joseph ALEXANDER and Esther Daniel, dau. Samuel Daniel who is surety with Clement Read. p 5

6 March 1815. James R. ALLGOOD and Sallie Pollard, dau. William Pollard. Sur. William H. Davis. James son of Samuel Allgood. p 535

24 July 1805. Perrin ALIDAY and Anne B. Tankersley (widow). Sur. William Price. p 371

16 December 1807. Edward C. ALLEN and Julia Brent, dau. James Brent. Sur. John Vawter. Married 19 December by Rev. John H. Rice. p 404

19 August 1794. Woodson ALLEN and Annis Palmer. Sur. Luke Palmer. p 207

1 February 1808. Edward O. ALMOND and Elizabeth Pettus, dau. Thomas Pettus. Sur. Edward Almond. p 418

24 October 1796. Hezekiah ALMOND and Polly Lee, dau. John Lee. Sur. Ambrose Haley. p 234

11 October 1791. Reuben ALMOND and Sarah Harris, dau. Charles Harris. Sur. William Hines. p 166

2 December 1794. Charles ANDERSON and Drucilla Jackson. Sur. John Vaughter. Charles son of William Anderson. Married 3 December by Rev. John Weatherford. p 207

4 October 1785. James ANDERSON and Sukey Brown, dau. Russell Brown who is surety. Married 5 October by Rev. John Weatherford. p 79

6 December 1813. Sterling C. ANDERSON and Anne W. Spencer, dau. Samuel S. Spencer. Sur. John Marshall. p 498

18 November 1793. James ANION and Mary Fore. Sur. John Fore. Married 20 November by Rev. William Mahon who says Molly Fore. p 195

17 June 1800. Micajah ARMES and Polly McDowell. Married by Rev. Joshua Worley. Ministers' Returns p 27

25 January 1786. James ARBUCKLE and Nancy Coleman, dau. Daniel Coleman. Sur. Thomas Hampton. p 84

14 February 1809. John ARMISTEAD and Clarissa White, ward of Nathan Harvey who is surety. p 438

21 September 1812. Samuel ARMISTEAD and Nancy Madison, dau. Martha Madison. Sur. C. C. H. Henderson. p 482

3 December 1787. James ARNOLD and Fanny Green, dau. John Green. Sur. Benjamin Green. Married 4 December by Rev. Thomas Johnston. p 100

17 February 1800. James ARNOLD and Uraney Wingo (widow). Sur. William Blake. Married 20 February by Rev. Edward Almond who says James Arnold Sen. and Mary Wingo. p 293

9 July 1789. Thomas ARNOLD and Jemima Eudaly, dau. John Eudaly. Sur. Thomas Smith. Married same day by Rev. Thomas Johnston who says Sarah Eudaley. p 135

20 November 1813. Thomas ARNOLD and Polly Green, dau. Benjamin Green. Sur. Adam Loving. Married same day by Rev. William Fears. p 498

- July 1788. Miller ASHWORTH and Mary Ann Ashworth. Married by Rev. David Ellington. See William Ashworth. Ministers' Returns p 9

16 February 1791. Harrison ASHWORTH and Elizabeth Ford. Sur. Henry
Ford. Married 13 March by Rev. John Williams. p 159

1 August 1796. Joel ASHWORTH and Milly Brizendine, dau. William Brizendine. Sur. William Ashworth. Married 3 August by Rev. Edward Almond.
p 233

22 June 1792. John ASHWORTH and Susannah Brizendine, dau. William
Brizendine. Sur. Mitchell Gill. Married 28 June by Rev. John
Williams. p 174

9 December 1804. Samuel ASHWORTH and Elizabeth Brizendine, dau. William
Brizendine. Sur. Travis Brooks. Married same day by Rev. William
Richards. p 359

2 January 1788. William ASHWORTH and Mary Ann Ashworth, dau. Samuel
Ashworth. Sur. John Ashworth. See Miller Ashworth. p 119

17 March 1806. Joseph ATKINS and Peggy Osborne, dau. Thomas Osborne.
Sur. John Atkins. Married 24 April by Rev. James Elmore. p 397

29 January 1774. William ATKINS and Anne Epperson, dau. Fran. Epperson.
Sur. John Smith. Wit. Thomas Epperson. p 23

17 February 1808. William ATKINS and Margaret Rudd. Sur. Thomas Rudd.
Married 18 February by Rev. John Chappell. p 428

3 May 1813. William ATWELL and Elizabeth Davis, dau. John Davis. Sur.
Joseph Davis. p 498

1 November 1813. Stephen AUSTIN and Elizabeth Berkeley, dau. George
Berkeley. Sur. James North. Married 18 November by Rev. Joshua
Worley. p 497

19 April 1799. William AVERILL and Betsey Hamlett, dau. James Hamlett.
Sur. Zachariah Sims. Married 20 April by Rev. Edward Almond. p 283½

4 October 1802. Lydall BACON and Peggy Crenshaw, ward of Ephraim
Bouldin. Sur. Hillery Moseley. p 323

4 November 1805. John G. BACON and Eliza Collier, ward of Thomas
Collier. Sur. Collier Hutcheson. John son of Langston Bacon.
Married same day by Rev. Thomas Hardie. p 371

13 July 1802. Andrew BAILEY and Polly Green, dau. John Green. Sur.
Croxton Green. p 325

11 April 1793. David BAILEY and Elizabeth Smith. Sur. William Scates.
p 193

4 October 1813. John BAILEY and Lucy Palmer, dau. Luke Palmer. Sur.
Charloss Wood. Married 14 October by Rev. John Chappell. p 507

22 August 1796. Presley BAILEY and Nancy Cayce. Sur. Micajah Cayce.
Married 23 August by Rev. John Chappell. p 233

23 December 1788. Robert BAILEY and Lucy Smith, dau. John Smith. Sur.
William T. Smith. p 119

15 January 1794. Brooks BAKER and Elizabeth King. Sur. Abner Baker.
Married 23 January by Rev. Henry Laster. p 209

7 February 1782. James BAKER and Elizabeth Fuqua, dau. William Fuqua.
Sur. Martin Baker. Married 14 February by Rev. Thomas Johnston. p 46

1 December 1785. Benjamin BALDWIN and Sarah Garden, dau. James Garden.
Sur. Thomas Baldwin. See Benjamin Bauldin. p 80

11 June 1807. Benjamin BALDWIN and Ann Sterling Thornton, dau. Francis
Thornton. Sur. Ralph Merriman. Benjamin son of William Baldwin.
Married 18 June by Rev. Drury Lacy. p 403

18 January 1806. William G. BAPTIST, Jr. and Elizabeth May, widow of
Stephen May. William G. son of William G. Baptist, Sr. Married by
Rev. Thomas Hardie. p 398

4 September 1786. Abner BARKSDALE and Betsey Garrett, dau. James
Garrett. Sur. John Barksdale. p 92

10 May 1778. Claiborne BARKSDALE and Jean Carter (widow). Sur. Dudley
Barksdale. p 31

6 February 1786. Dudley BARKSDALE and Elizabeth Wimbish (widow). Sur.
William Morton. Married 15 February by Rev. John Weatherford. p 90

6 February 1810. Grief BARKSDALE and Mary A. Elliott, ward of Charles
Raine. Sur. Claiborne Barksdale, Jr. p 452

16 November 1791. William BARKSDALE and Nancy Harrison (widow). Sur.
Daniel Barksdale. p 157

9 October 1802. Samuel BARLEY and Betsey High, dau. David High. Sur.
Westmoreland High. p 323

26 August 1772. Francis BARNES and Anne Osborne, dau. Reps. Osborne.
Sur. James Barnes. p 15

23 December 1791. Francis BARNES, Jr. and Lucy Cargill. Sur. John
Barnes. Francis, Jr. son of Francis Barnes, Sr. Married 25
December by Rev. John Williams. p 167

16 December 1788. Gabriel BARNES and Lucy Ann Stow, dau. Joel and
Susanna Stow. Sur. Benjamin Cheatham. p 118

16 Mary 1803. George BARNES and Susanna Lockett, widow of Thomas
Lockett. Sur. James Barnes. Married 19 May by Rev. Edward Almond.
p 334

20 April 1782. Henry BARNES and Margaret Caldwell Wood. Married by
Rev. John Weatherford. Ministers' Returns p 3

2 January 1796. John BARNES and Elizabeth Cage. Sur. Lemuel Stowe.
p 247

24 January 1806. Leonard BARNES and Mary Gaines, dau. William Gaines
who is surety. Leonard son of Gabriel Barnes. Married same day by
Rev. Richard Dabbs, Jr. p 398

5 March 1810. William BARNES and Polly Wheeler, dau. William Wheeler
who is surety. p 451

9 September 1811. William BAPTIST and Elizabeth May. Sur. Richard Russell. p 474

10 October 1798. Thomas BARRETT and Judith Wilkes. Sur. William Wilkes. p 267

12 February 1800. David BARTEE and Sally Sims, dau. Richard Sims. Sur. Benjamin Hudson. p 288

24 January 1801. John BARTEE and Nanney Parker, dau. William Parker. Sur. William Davis. See John Barlow. p 312

23 October 1784. George BARTLEY and Sally Wheeler. Married by Rev. John Weatherford. See George Berkeley. Ministers' Returns p 3

22 July 1787. Robert BARTON and Nancy Whitlock. Married by Rev. Thomas Johnston. See Robert Burton. Ministers' Returns p 7

27 January 1801. John BARTOW and Nancy Parker. Married by Rev. Obadiah Edge. See John Bartee. Ministers' Returns p 25

4 December 1797. Nathan BASEBEACH and Patsey Day. Sur. Thomas Toombs. p 246

26 March 1790. John BASSETT and Nancy Comer. Sur. William Bryant. Married 27 March by Rev. Edward Almond. p 142

6 August 1797. John BAUGTHON and Jean Hunter. Sur. Richard Davenport. p 266

14 March 1812. John B. BEACH and Elizabeth Toombs, dau. Thomas Toombs. Sur. Henry Worsham. p 490

4 September 1809. John BEADLES and Sarah Adams, dau. James Adams. Sur. James Brent. Married 7 September by Rev. Richard Dabbs. p 433

6 December 1802. Lewis BEADLES and Martha Vaughan, consent of Nicholas Vaughan. Sur. George W. Baldwin. p 322

3 March 1789. Cornelius BEASLEY and Edith Towler. Sur. Cain Jackson. Married 5 March by Rev. Thomas Johnston. p 135

4 January 1804. Ephraim BEASLEY and Elizabeth Coleman Hart, dau. William Hart who is surety. Ephraim son of Gabriel Beasley. p 350

26 September 1786. Benjamin BEDFORD and Tabitha Clay. Married by Rev. Thomas Johnston. Ministers' Returns p 7

6 February 1783. Robert BEDFORD and Mary Hill Read, dau. M. Read. Sur. James Hamlett. Robert son of Stephen Bedford, deceased. Married 27 February by the Rev. Thomas Johnston. p 55

8 January 1793. Stephen BEDFORD and Jane Daniel. Sur. John Daniel, Jr. Married 10 January by Rev. William Mahon. p 192

5 March 1810. Obadiah BELCHER and Sally Blanks. Sur. George Calhoun. Married 25 March by Rev. William Richards. p 451

2 November 1782. George BERKELEY and Sally Wheeler, dau. John Wheeler
    who is surety. George son of Alexander Berkeley. See George
    Bartley. p 52

7 December 1802. John BERKELEY and Jane (Jeane) Moore. Sur. Charles
    McKinney. Married 8 December by Rev. Joshua Worley. p 324

23 June 1795. Charles BERRIMAN and Nancy Haney. Sur. John Smith. p 221

20 January 1796. George BEVERLY and Judith Jennings. Married by Rev.
    William Mahon. See George Reverly. Ministers' Returns p 20

9 December 1782. John BEVENEER (?) and Polly Martin. Married by Rev.
    John Weatherford. Ministers' Returns p 3

6 August 1804. Branch BIBB and Lucy Scott, dau. John Scott. Sur.
    Robert Morton. Married 9 August by Rev. Joshua Worley. p 349

1 November 1802. John BIBB and Susanna Marshall, dau. William Marshall.
    Sur. John Holcombe, Jr. Married 2 November by Rev. Joshua Worley.
    p 329

1 August 1796. Philemon H. BIBB and Martha Fuqua. Sur. Hillery Moseley.
    Married 18 August by Rev. Edward Almond. p 232

6 August 1792. William BIBB and Mary A. Thompson (widow). Sur. Edward
    Moseley. Married 11 September by Rev. John Williams. p 169

27 March 1805. Burwell BIGGS and Elizabeth Lambert, dau. of Sterling
    Lambert who is surety. p 372

17 October 1801. Freeman BIGGS and Lucretia Williams, dau. Robert
    Williams who is surety. Freeman son of John Biggs. Married
    29 October by Rev. Thomas Dobson. p 312

4 January 1808. Peter BIGGS and Polly Wright, dau. Ester Wright. Sur.
    James Hinge. Married 17 January by Rev. William Fears. p 415

28 August 1793. Willis BIGGS and Mary Williams. Married by Rev. Thomas
    Dobson. See Willis Diggs. Ministers' Returns p 16

11 July 1810. Benjamin BILBRO and Penelope Chaney. Sur. James Chaney.
    p 452

2 April 1783. John BILLUPS and Frances Bedford, dau. Robert Bedford.
    Sur. William Hamlett. John Billups from Lunenburg County. (Note: I
    think she was dau. of Stephen Bedford and sister of Robert Bedford.
    Both mentioned in Stephen's will 1772.) Married 3 April by Rev.
    Thomas Johnston. p 55

19 November 1796. William BIRD and Polly Carter, dau.-in-law (step-dau?)
    of William Brogdon. Sur. John Chavus. Married 22 November by Rev.
    Thomas Dobson. (William Brogdon was a Negro. This bond does not
    designate race or color.) p 233

16 May 1799. Peter BIRTHRIGHT and Patsey McIndoe, dau. Nancy Brown.
    Sur. Jeremiah Brown, Jr. Peter son of Zachariah Birthright.
    Married same day by Rev. John Chappell. p 284

13 January 1790. Frederick BLACK and Elizabeth Lockett. Married by
    Rev. John Williams. Ministers' Returns p 11

3 January 1803. John BLACK and Rebecca Newman Sandifer. Sur. Robert
Robeson. p 335

27 October 1788. William BLACK and Polly Jordan, dau. Matthew Jordan.
Sur. William Bryant. Married 30 October by Rev. Joshua Worley. p 119

10 October 1800. Lemerie Williams BLAKE and Lucy Bradberry, dau.
William Bradberry who is surety. p 289

5 November 1799. William BLAKE, Jr. and Elizabeth Pollard. Sur. Adam
Levin. Married 7 November by Rev. Edward Almond. p 284

12 June 1781. Samuel BLAND and Elizabeth Williamson, dau. Cuthbert
Williamson who is surety. p 42

2 February 1794. Andrew BLANKENSHIP and Margaret Bardin, dau. Nancy
Bardin. Sur. William Leafman. Married same day by Rev. Edward
Almond. p 209

29 November 1786. Levy BLANKENSHIP and Millinder Calvert, dau. Nelson
Calvert who is surety. Married by Rev. David Ellington. p 84

30 December 1810. Nathan BLANKENSHIP and Martha Green. Married by
Rev. David McCargo. See Naum Blankenship. Ministers' Returns p 40

29 December 1810. Naum BLANKENSHIP and Martha Green. Sur. John Nance.
See Nathan Blankenship. p 451

6 February 1804. John BLANKS and Elizabeth Finch, widow of John Finch.
Sur. Thomas Finch. Married 23 February by Rev. Edward Almond. p 349

4 May 1807. John BLANKS and Nancy Moseley (widow). Sur. John Howell.
p 402

1 October 1781. Shadrock BLANKS and Lydia Perrin, dau. Joseph Perrin.
Sur. John Bridges. p 44

6 November 1798. Benjamin BOLEY and Patience W. Daniel. Sur. Prestly
Boley. Married 15 November by Rev. John Chappell. p 266

18 June 1804. Prestley BOLEY and Polly W. Daniel, dau. James Daniel.
Sur. Seth Ward. Married 20 June by Rev. John Chappell. p 349

3 October 1782. Michael BOLLING and Elizabeth Littlepage. Married by
Rev. John Weatherford. Ministers' Returns p 2

21 February 1791. Moses BOND and Elizabeth Hubbard, dau. Thomas Hubbard.
Sur. William Hutcheson. Married 24 February by Rev. John Williams
who says Winney Hubbard. p 163

4 July 1803. John S. BOOKER and Martha Harris, dau. Robert Harris.
Sur. Robert Harris, Jr. Married 21 July by Rev. John Chappell. p 334

20 October 1789. Parham BOOKER and Polly Spencer, dau. Gideon Spencer.
Sur. John Nash Read. Married 22 October by Rev. William Mahon. p 133

2 February 1795. Richard BOOKER and Tabitha Fuqua. Sur. Thomas Mackey.
p 222

17 June 1797. Richard BOOKER and Ridley Jones. Sur. William Wyatt.
Married 13 July by Rev. John Chappell. p 247

28 November 1785. Benjamin BOULDIN and Sarah Gordon or Gardon. Married
by Rev. John Weatherford. See Benjamin Baldwin. Ministers' Returns
p 5

1 September 1794. Ephraim BOULDIN and Jincey Flippen Bedford, dau.
Thomas Bedford, deceased. Sur. James Collier. Married 3 September
by Rev. John Williams. p 207

20 November 1808. James BOULDIN and Betsey Bouldin, dau. Richard
Bouldin who is surety. Married 1 December by Rev. John H. Rice. p 415

7 December 1813. James W. BOULDIN and Aloe Jonitt. James son of Thomas
T. Bouldin who is surety. p 512

17 September 1789. John BOULDIN and Elizabeth St. John, dau. Elizabeth
St. John. Sur. Abraham St. John. Married 20 September by Rev. John
Weatherford. p 131

2 April 1777. Wood BOULDINE and Joanna Tyler. Sur. Thomas Read. p 28

2 August 1778. Thomas BOWER and Liddia Mullins. p 31

2 August 1778. Thomas BOWERS and Lydia Cullins, dau. Elizabeth Grayson.
Sur. Edward Russell. (Evidently the same as above.) p 32

7 November 1780. Robert BOWMAN and Sarah Foster, dau. James Foster.
Sur. Joshua Foster. p 39

23 February 1812. William BRADBERRY and Sukey Haley. Married by Rev.
William Fears. Ministers' Returns p 41

22 February 1813. William BRADBERRY and Sukey Haley, dau. Pleasant
Haley who is surety. p 497

4 October 1802. John BRADLEY and Mary Weatherford, dau. Joseph
Weatherford. Sur. Dr. F. Fuqua. Married 14 October by Rev. Edward
Almond. p 325

25 December 1802. Samuel BRAFFORD and Betsey Newcomb, dau. Charles
Newcomb who is surety. Married 20 January 1803 by Rev. Joshua Worley.
p 324

19 December 1812. William BRAGG and Nancy Almond, dau. Elish Almond.
Sur. Absolom Tatum. Married 22 December by Rev. James Robertson. p 482

4 May 1807. Thomas BRANCH and Mariah Berkeley North, dau. Thomas North
who is surety. Married 20 May by Rev. Joshua Worley. p 402

3 January 1794. Moses BRANDUM and Alley Jackson. Sur. John Chavus. p 210

3 September 1765. John BREEDLOVE and Elizabeth Watkins, dau. William
Watkins. Sur. Ezekiah Jackson. p 2

28 November 1804. Nathaniel BREEDLOVE and Polly Watkins, dau. Benjamin
Watkins. Sur. William Watkins. p 350

5 July 1782. Thomas BRISCO and Elizabeth Tackett. Married by Rev. John Weatherford. Ministers' Returns p 2

5 May 1772. John BRIDGES and Mary Ligon, dau. Thomas Ligon. Sur. James Sullivant. p 15

22 April 1801. Banister BRIZENDINE and Tabitha Whitlow, dau. Anne Whitlow. Sur. John Ashworth. Married 4 May by Rev. Edward Almond. p 311

10 November 1798. Isaac BRIZENDINE and Polly Brizendine, dau. Isaac Brizendine. Sur. Bibby Brooks. Married 11 November by Rev. Edward Almond. p 266

22 December 1802. John BRIZENDINE and Dicey Hall. Sur. Miles Bottom. Married 29 December by Rev. Edward Almond. p 324

15 August 1804. Langford BRIZENDINE and Elizabeth Hall. Langford son of William Brizendine. Sur. John Brizendine. Married 18 August by Rev. William Richards. p 360

16 January 1815. Richard BRIZENDINE and Sallie Adams, dau. William Adams. Sur. W. E. Spraggins. Richard son of Reuben Brizendine. Married by Rev. Joshua Worley. p 532

14 August 1797. William BRIZENDINE, Jr. and Milley Lindsay, dau. Wright Lindsey. Sur. Joel Ashworth. William son of William Brizendine. Married 17 August by Rev. Edward Almond. p 247

2 February 1813. William BRIZENDINE and Anne Clark, dau. Thomas Clark. Sur. Richard Clark. p 505

9 November 1803. Young BRIZENDINE and Ann Ritter Herndon, dau. Joseph Herndon. Sur. Richard Brizendine. Married same day by Rev. William Richards. p 331

7 February 1809. James BROOKE and Sally Going, dau. Thomas Going. Sur. John Going. Married 18 February by Rev. William Fears. p 433

14 November 1800. Thomas BROOKE and Elizabeth Raine, dau. John Raine. Sur. Lydal Bacon. Married 19 November by Rev. Edward Almond who says Rains. p 289

6 March 1804. Zachariah BROOKE and Fanny Overby, dau. Richard Overby. Sur. James Cheaney. p 361

22 November 1802. David BROOKS and Mary Marable, dau. Elizabeth Marable. Sur. Champion Marable (brother). David son of Joel and Patty Brooks. Married 23 November by Rev. Edward Almond. p 323

20 November 1797. Elijah BROOKS and Frances Marable, dau. Lisbeth Marable. Sur. John Rawlins. Elijah son of Joel Brooks. Married 21 November by Rev. Edward Almond. p 248

15 February 1814. Hezekiah BROOKS and Elizabeth Rowlett, dau. Mackerness Rowlett. Sur. John Rowlett. Married 17 February by Rev. James Robinson. p 518

2 December 1799. James BROOKS and Betsey H. Watkins, dau. Ben Watkins.
Sur. William Childress. p 283½

7 June 1802. John BROOKS and Betsey West Brooke, dau. Amos West Brooke.
Sur. Reuben Palmer. p 325

7 October 1799. Levi BROOKS and Nancy Hamblin, dau. Mack and Mary
Hamblin. Sur. Edward Hamblin. Lewi son of Joel Brooks. Married
16 October by Rev. Edward Almond. p 285

1 September 1806. Travis BROOKS and Elizabeth Moseley, dau. Arthur
Moseley. Sur. Hillary Moseley. Married 10 September by Rev.
Richard Dabbs, Jr. p 398

5 March 1807. Alexander BROWN and Nancy Mann. Sur. Jesse Mann.
Married 6 March by Rev. David McCargo. p 402

14 January 1813. A. Burwell BROWN and Jinsey Haley, dau. Thomas Haley.
Sur. Henry Haley. Married 16 January by Rev. Richard Dabbs. p 505

25 December 1794. Burwell BROWN, Jr. and Betsey Sandifer, dau. John
Sandifer. Sur. Hubbard Williams. Married same day by Rev. John
Weatherford. p 209

19 October 1812. Charles V. BROWN and Elizabeth Akers, dau. Peter Akers.
Sur. John Harroway. p 481

19 March 1788. Eppa BROWN and Sabina Sallard, dau. William Sallard.
Sur. Rains Cook. Eppa son of Burwell Brown. Married 20 March by
Rev. Thomas Johnston. p 117

18 October 1788. Henry BROWN and Betsey Gaines, dau. Richard Gaines.
Sur. William Gaines. p 118

2 December 1813. Henry BROWN and Sally Brown, dau. James Brown who is
surety. p 507

30 November 1796. James BROWN and Patience Jackson. Sur. Joel
Sullivant. Married 8 December by Rev. John Chappell. p 232

2 May 1803. James BROWN and Elizabeth Adams, dau. James Adams who is
surety. p 335

13 March 1780. Jesse BROWN and Margaret Hatchett. Sur. Robert Bowman.
p 40

1 February 1779. John BROWN and Milly Gaines, dau. Richard Gaines who
is surety. p 34

29 June 1790. Nicholas BROWN and Molly Dunn. Sur. Edmund Dunn. p 141

2 November 1805. Oliver BROWN and Patience Bailey, dau. Mary Bailey.
Sur. John Johnson. p 372

21 October 1792. Richard BROWN and Jenny Hancock. Sur. Samuel Pryor.
Returned January Court 1793 by Rev. John Chappell. Jenny dau.
Anthony Hancock. p 171

5 February 1799. Russell BROWN and Fanny Birthright, dau. Zachariah
Birthright. Sur. Peter Birthright. Russell son of Mary Brown.
Married 7 February by Rev. John Chappell. p 279

5 April 1805. Russell BROWN and Sophia Marks. Sur. Joshua Nichols.
p 373

22 May 1804. Thomas BROWN and Martha Daniel, dau. John Daniel. Sur.
Stephen Bedford. p 360

2 December 1782. William BROWN and Catherine Ward, dau. John Ward. Sur.
Valentine Smith. Married 3 December by Rev. Thomas Johnston. p 50

1 April 1793. William BROWN and Polly Warren. Sur. Russell Brown.
Married by Rev. John Chappell. Returned to the May Court 1793. p 192

28 June 1775. John BRUCE and Elizabeth Clay, dau. Henry Clay. Sur.
John Clay. p 27

24 September 1801. Nelson BRUCE and Susanna Roberson. Sur. Archie
Farley. Married 1 October by Rev. William Richards. p 311

15 December 1789. John BRYAN and Anne Steep (?). Married by Rev. John
Weatherford. Ministers' Returns p 12

15 January 1797. Burwell BRYANT and Agnes Armes, dau. Edward Armes who
is surety. Married 24 January by Rev. Joshua Worley. p 246

2 March 1812. John C. BRYANT and Martha Ryon, dau. William Ryon. Sur.
John Freeman. Married 21 March by Rev. George Petty. p 490

6 September 1794. Josiah BRYANT and Polly Lipton. Sur. Joseph Reynolds.
Josiah Bryant of Prince Edward County, son of Mary Bryant. Married
8 October by Rev. John Williams who says Polly Sexton (or Saxton).
p 208

11 December 1784. William BRYANT and Sarah Kennady, dau. John Kennady.
Sur. Joseph Wood. Married same day by Rev. Thomas Johnston. p 63

9 October 1804. William BRYANT and Elizabeth Harris. Sur. Jeremiah
Walker. Married 11 October by Rev. Richard Dabbs, Jr. p 361

2 July 1798. Nathan BUCKLEY and Polly Lipscomb. Sur. Richard G.
Lipscomb. p 274

28 July 1792. Henry BUCKNER, Jr. and Elizabeth Womack, dau. Alexander
Womack. Sur. John Foster. Henry, Jr. son of Henry Buckner, Sr.
Married 30 July by Rev. Henry Lester. p 171

20 June 1774. Diggs BUMPASS and Frances Bedford, widow of Stephen
Bedford. (Will 4 June 1772). Sur. John Williams. p 24

27 April 1780. Jesse BUNKLEY and Alley Barksdale. Sur. William Davis.
p 37

16 September 1796. William BURCHETT and Sally Roberts. Sur. Edmund
Osborne. Married 19 September by Rev. Edward Almond. p 232

2 December 1799. John BURCHFIELD and Amy Sublett, dau. William Sublett.
Sur. William Sublett. Married 5 December by Rev. John Chappell. p 284

2 April 1787. George BURKS and Mildred Hatchett, dau. John Hatchett.
Sur. Richard Burks. Married 11 April by Rev. Archibald McRoberts. p108

8 July 1782. Henry BURLEY and Lucy Davenport. Married by Rev. John Weatherford. See Henry Burnley. Ministers' Returns p 2

10 September 1804. Harrison BURNES and Judith Fuqua, dau. John Fuqua who is surety. Married 14 September by Rev. Edward Almond. p 350

13 July 1782. Henry BURNLEY and Lucy Davenport (widow), daughter-in-law of Richard Davenport who is surety. See Henry Burley. p 48

1 September 1804. William BURNS and Sally May (widow). Sur. Joseph Pearson. Married same day by Rev. Richard Dabbs, Jr. p 351

17 December 1782. John BURRASS and Elizabeth Elam, dau. William Elam. Sur. Martin Elam. Married 19 December by Rev. Thomas Johnston. p 49

26 January 1785. Isaac BURTON and Sally Bolling. Married by Rev. John Weatherford. Ministers' Returns p 3

4 August 1788. John BURTON and Polly Webster, dau. Charles Webster. Sur. Samuel Burton. Married 6 August by Rev. John Williams. p 117

21 February 1787. Robert BURTON and Nancy Whitlock, dau. Charles Whitlock who is surety. See Robert Barton. p 107

12 November 1789. Samuel BURTON and Patty Hutcheson, dau. Watt W. Hutcheson. Sur. William Hutcheson. Married 13 November by Rev. John Williams. p 128

14 March 1812. John B. BUSH and Elizabeth Toombs. Married by Rev. James Robertson. Ministers' Returns p 40

5 September 1808. William BUSTER and Elizabeth P. Marshall, dau. Benjamin Marshall. Sur. John Buster. p 414

5 October 1782. John BUTLER and Elizabeth Nicholson. Married by Rev. John Weatherford. Ministers' Returns p 2

20 August 1790. Joseph BYRD and Nettie Jackson. Sur. Burwell Jackson. p 144

7 April 1795. Fielder CAGE and Susanna Jones. Sur. Richard Booker. Married 15 April by Rev. Charles Cobbs. p 221

21 August 1814. Jesse CAGE and Anne Davis, dau. Joseph Davis. Sur. Gabriel Barnes. Married 23 August by Rev. Richard Dabbs, Jr. p 362

5 January 1803. John CAGE and Peggy Barnes, widow of Henry Barnes. Sur. James Adams. Married 6 January by Rev. John Chappell. p 331

28 May 1770. Samuel CALDWELL and Sarah Cunningham, dau. James Cunningham. Sur. Robert Caldwell. p 9

6 June 1803. George CALHOUN and Susanna G. Coleman, dau. James Coleman. Sur. Isham Chastain. p 348

14 February 1788. James CALHOUN and Martha Claybrook, dau. Obadiah Claybrook who is surety. Married 28 April by Rev. John B. Smith. p 112

14 June 1792. James CALLICOT and Susanna Brooke (widow). Sur. William Callicot. Married 19 June by Rev. John Williams. p 183

20 December 1791. William CALLICOTT and Elizabeth Ashworth, dau. Samuel Ashworth. Sur. Beverley Callicott. Married 22 December by Rev. John Williams. P 158

1 September 1773. John CAMERON and Anne Owen Nash. Sur. Thomas Read. p 18

13 November 1812. James CAMMELL and Lucy Wingo, dau. Raney (Uraney) Arnold. Sur. Adam Loving. Married 14 November by Rev. William Fears. p 486

27 November 1797. George CAMP and Frances Hudson, dau. Daniel and Tabitha Hudson. Sec. Jacob Hudson. Married 29 November by Rev. William Richards. p 248

3 November 1800. Lewis CAMP and Joanna Neal, dau. Thomas Neal who is surety. Married 6 November by Rev. Edward Almond. p 292

26 November 1787. Archibald CAMPBELL and Margaret Arnold, dau. James Arnold. Sur. Edmund Keeling. Married 27 November by Rev. David Ellington. p 111

6 July 1795. Archibald CAMPBELL and Susanna Muntford, dau. James H. Muntford. Sur. William Barnes. Married 9 July by Rev. John Chappell. p 223

31 August 1799. Robert CAMPBELL and Sarah Butler Henry, dau. Patrick and Dorathea Henry. Sur. John D. Johnson. p 286

3 December 1792. Willshire CARDWELL and Mary Russell, dau. Edmund Russell. Sur. Thomas Epperson. Married 18 December by Rev. Archibald McRobert. p 177

7 August 1815. Wyatt CARDWELL and Patsey Cary, dau. William H. Cary. Sur. Joseph Davis. p 525

19 December 1803. Clement CARRINGTON and Jane Poage (widow). Sur. Thomas Read. Married same day by Rev. Drury Lacy. p 345

4 September 1788. George CARRINGTON and Anna Hughs Williams, dau. Rev. John Williams. Sur. Matthew Williams. Married 15 September by Rev. John Williams. p 114

10 June 1811. Robert CARSON and Elizabeth Mullins. Sur. James Mullins. Married 4 July by Rev. Bernard Todd. p 473

25 October 1786. Charles CARTER and Lucy Barksdale, dau. Dudley Barksdale. Sur. Caleb Townes. p 87

2 June 1794. Coleman CARTER and Elizabeth Smith. Sur. Woodley Holt. Married 8 June by Rev. Edward Almond. p 210

11 March 1807. Crafford CARTER and Molly Loggins, dau. Martin Loggins who is surety. Married 18 March by Rev. Richard Dabbs, Jr. p 401

5 July 1768. John CARTER and Jean Morton, dau. Joseph Morton. Sur. Thomas Read. p 6

13

28 March 1810. Michael CARTER and Jane Hailey, dau. John Hailey. Sur. Robert Williams. p 461

31 July 1801. Richard CARTER and Sally Fuqua. Sur. Dr. F. Fuqua. Married by Rev. Edward Almond. p 314

26 November 1774. Robert CARTER and Patty Barksdill. Sur. James Carter. p 23

31 July 1800. Samuel CARTER and Susanna Bibb, dau. John Bibb. Sur. Josiah Moseley. p 292

8 September 1794. Robertson CARWILES and Lucy Roach. Sur. William Roach. Married 9 September by Rev. Joshua Worley. p 208

3 November 1810. Archibald CARY and Patsey Johnson, dau. William Johnson who is surety. Married 8 November by Rev. Richard Dabbs. p 453

2 January 1809. Richard CARY and Rebecca Johnson, dau. William Johnson who is surety. Married 5 January by Rev. John H. Rice. p 434

29 January 1802. William Haynes CARY and Esther Jackson, dau. Thomas Jackson. Sur. John Jackson, Jr. p 328·

24 October 1796. Micajah CAYCE and Mary Ward. Sur. Seth Ward. Married 25 October by Rev. Thomas Dobson. p 234

5 December 1803. Micajah CAYCE and Nancy Smith, dau. Thomas Smith who is surety. p 343

23 November 1791. Pleasant CAYSE and Ann Claybrook, dau. Obodiah Claybrook. Sur. Peter Claybrook. Married 1 December by Rev. Drury Lacy. p 158

4 March 1805. Anderson CHAFFIN and Frances Vaughan, dau. William Vaughan who is surety. Anderson son of Joseph Chaffin. p 374

19 December 1810. Archer CHAFFIN and Frances Fears, dau. William Fears who is surety. p 453

17 December 1805. Coleman CHAFFIN and Susanna Weatherford, dau. Samuel Weatherford. Sur. Thomas Chaffin. Married 19 December by Rev. Edward Almond. p 371

6 December 1802. John CHAFFIN and Tabitha Chaffin. Married by Rev. Edward Almond. Ministers' Returns p 30

15 June 1793. Nathan CHAFFIN and Elizabeth Sweeney, dau. Mary Sweeney. Sur. Joshua Chaffin. Married 10 July by Rev. Edward Almond, who says Swinney. p 205

24 December 1811. Nathan CHAFFIN and Harriet Hatchett, dau. Thomas Hatchett. Sur. Austin Clements. p 474

25 March 1803. Thomas CHAFFIN, Jr. and Nancy Mayse, dau. William Mayse. Sur. Thomas Chaffin, Sr. Married 17 March (?) by Rev. Edward Almond who says Mayes. p 343

2 September 1805. James CHANDLER and Susanna Alderson, ward of James Alderson. Sur. William Chandler. James son of Thomas Chandler. p 373

4 February 1806. John CHASTAIN and Polly Bottom. Married by Rev. James
Elmore. See John Christian. Ministers' Returns p 34

27 January 1786. Thomas CHAVUS and Nancy Thaxton. Sur. William Dabbs.
Married 3 February by Rev. Thomas Johnston. p 90

7 October 1805. Ambrose CHEANEY and Polly Rawlins. Sur. Thomas Cheaney.
Married same day by Rev. Thomas Hardie. p 373

18 December 1804. Henry CHEANEY and Mary Goode Barnes, dau. Francis
Barnes, Sr. Sur. Francis Barnes, Jr. Married 20 December by Rev.
Edward Almond. p 361

21 November 1801. Heritage CHEANEY and Peggy Johnson, dau. Sias Johnson
who is surety. Heritage son of Thomas Cheaney. p 312

7 September 1801. John CHEANEY and Mary Dupree, dau. William Dupree.
Sur. James Cheaney. p 313

23 April 1800. Reuben CHEANEY and Julia Dupree, dau. William Dupree.
Sur. James Cheaney. Married 24 April by Rev. Edward Almond. p 292

24 September 1800. William CHEANEY, Jr. and Martha Brooke, dau. Dudley
Brooke. Sur. Thomas Cheaney. William son of William Cheaney, Sr.
Married 25 September by Rev. Edward Almond. p 291

2 November 1789. Arthur CHEATHAM and Nancy Hancock. Sur. Isaac Smith.
Married 5 November by Rev. John Weatherford. p 130

5 December 1791. Bernard CHEATHAM and Judith Hampton. Sur. James Brent.
Married 10 December by Rev. Edward Almond. p 163

6 January 1806. Joseph CHEATHAM and Elizabeth Beasley (widow). Sur.
Richard Hunt (Hart?). Married 9 January by Rev. Richard Dabbs, Jr.
p 396

8 November 1785. William CHEATHAM and Nancy Clark Smith. Sur. Joseph
Reis. Married 10 November by Rev. Thomas Johnston who says Nancy
Clark. p 67

4 August 1795. Drury CHILDRESS and Phoebe Bowles. Sur. John Robertson.
p 223

5 November 1792. Jeremiah CHILDRESS and Nancy Vaughan, dau. Abraham and
Nannie Vaughan. Sur. John Vaughan. See Jeremiah Childrey. p 177

5 February 1781. John CHILDRESS and Nancy Ferrell, dau. William Ferrell.
Sur. James Duncan. p 45

6 December 1813. John CHILDRESS and Elizabeth Berkeley. Sur. Charles
McKinney. p 508

17 December 1813. John CHILDRESS and Elizabeth Parsons. Married by
Rev. Joshua Worley. Ministers' Returns p 44

27 October 1786. William CHILDRESS and Anne Hanson (Henson). Married
by Rev. Thomas Johnston. See William Childrey. Ministers' Returns
p 7

25 November 1794. William CHILDRESS and Peggy Hazelwood, dau. William
Hazelwood who is surety. Married 27 November by Rev. Obodiah Edge. p 210

8 October 1799. William CHILDRESS and Patty Breedlove, dau. John and Elizabeth Breedlove. Sur. William B. Breedlove. Married 9 October by Rev. Drury Lacy. p 285

7 November 1792. Jeremiah CHILDREY and Nancy Vaughan. Married by Rev. Edward Almond. See Jeremiah Childress. Ministers' Returns p 12

27 December 1786. William CHILDREY and Anne Henson, dau. Elizabeth Henson. Sur. James Foster. See William Childress. p 94

7 December 1812. John CHISM and Sally Parker, dau. Martha Parker. Sur. John M. Bartee. p 489

17 March 1789. Obodiah CHISOLM and Mary Ann Cardwell, dau. Richard and Susanna Cardwell. Sur. Francis Jackson. Married 18 March by Rev. William Mahon. p 133

3 July 1809. Archibald CHOCKLEY (or CHECKLEY) and Sally R. Palmer, dau. Halcote Palmer who is surety. p 434

3 February 1806. John CHRISTIAN and Polly Bottom, dau. Miles Bottom. Sur. John Howell. See John Chastain. p 395

28 December 1780. Edward CLARK and Sarah Hight, dau. John Hight. Sur. William Smith. p 41

6 December 1784. Elijah CLARK and Mary Jackson, dau. Lewis Jackson who is surety. Married 20 January 1785, by Rev. Thomas Johnston. p 64

23 February 1811. James CLARK, Jr. and Polly Harris, dau. Robert Harris. Sur. Ezekiel Harris. Married 28 February by Rev. John Chappell. p 476

7 December 1812. James CLARK and Sally L. Harvey, dau. William Harvey. Sur. Harvey Paulett. Married 11 December by Rev. Joshua Worley. p 489

7 December 1792. John CLARK and Sally Watkins, dau. Benjamine Watkins. Sur. Richard Watkins. Married 13 December by Rev. Drury Lacy. p 171

9 September 1801. John E. CLARK and Elizabeth Scott. Married by Rev. Obodiah Edge. Ministers' Returns p 26

8 March 1813. Lewis CLARK and Nancy Jackson, dau. Thomas Jackson. Sur. Thomas Jackson, Jr. p 506

25 December 1792. Robert CLARK and Judith Weaver, dau. James Weaver. Sur. Meredith Walker. Married 3 January 1793 by Rev. William Mahon. p 179

22 March 1785. Thomas CLARK and Elizabeth Howard, dau. William Howard who is surety. Married 6 April by Rev. John Weatherford. p 67

4 December 1792. John CLARKSON and Frances Martin, dau. Sylla Martin. Sur. Joseph Clarkson. Married 6 December by Rev. Joshua Worley. p 178

2 May 1785. Joseph CLARKSON and Betsey Martin, dau. Richard Martin who is surety. Married 15 May by Rev. John Weatherford. p 67

7 January 1793. Josiah CLAYBROOK and Martha Johnson. Sur. Reuben Johnson. Married 10 January by Rev. Drury Lacy. p 204

18 November 1806. Thomas CLAYTON and Polly Anderson, dau. Worsham Anderson. Sur. John Huntsman. p 396

22 March 1785. Bernard CLEMENTS and Sally Givin. Sur. Matthew Williams. p 68

11 July 1797. Robert CLEMENTS and Charlotte Sweeney. Sur. Samuel Weatherford. Married 13 July by Rev. Edward Almond. p 260

2 October 1797. William Walton COBBS and Nancy Newton Brent. Sur. James Brent. William W. Cobbs of Campbell County and son of Charles Cobbs. p 249

27 February 1790. Benjamin COCKE and Suannah North. Married by Rev. John Weatherford. See Benjamin Cox. Ministers' Returns p 12

6 June 1808. William CODY and Polly Singleton Lumpkin, dau. James Lumpkin. Sur. John Bouldin. Married 9 June by Rev. Richard Dabbs, Jr. p 413

23 September 1774. James COLE, Jr. and Mary Lightfoot Russell (widow). Sur. Josiah Cole. p 22

18 August 1772. John COLE and Mary Wills. p 16

19 December 1814. Anderson COLEMAN and Sally S. Barnes, dau. Francis Barnes. Sur. John Coleman. Married 22 December by Rev. William Richards. p 520

23 December 1811. James COLEMAN and Nancy Brown, dau.-in-law (step-dau?) Thomas Gayle. Sur. Francis Barnes. p 473

7 February 1811. Isaac COLES, Jr. and Lightfoot Carrington, dau. Paul Carrington, Jr. Sur. Edward C. Carrington. Married same day by Rev. John H. Rice. p 474

15 November 1787. Benjamin COLLIER and Sarah Gaines Collier, dau. John Collier. Sur. Thomas Hudspeth. Married 20 November by Rev. John Williams. p 101

7 June 1802. Dabney COLLIER and Sarah Barksdale, dau. Claiborne Barksdale. Sur. William Gaines. p 327

4 October 1802. Hamlett COLLIER and Elizabeth Towler, dau. Japheth and Elizabeth Towler. Sur. James Cheaney. Married 7 October by Rev. Edward Almond. p 327

30 June 1788. James COLLIER and Betty Bouldin, dau. James Bouldin. Sur. John Collier. Married 3 July by Rev. John Williams. p 114

15 December 1772. Joseph COLLIER and Amey Moseley, dau. Edward Moseley. Sur. William Bouldin. p 16

3 March 1794. William Tompkins COLLIER and Betsey Williams. Sur. William Vaughan. Married 6 March by Rev. John Williams. p 211

15 August 1812. Elisha COLLINS and Catherine White, dau. William White. Sur. John White. p 489

3 January 1785. Joel COLLINS and Rhoda Chaffin, dau. Joshua Chaffin. Sur. Thomas Chaffin. Married 25 January by Rev. Thomas Johnston. p 78

14 December 1813. John COLLINS and Jane Weatherford, dau. Samuel Weatherford. Sur. William Wallace. John son of Joel Collins. p 506

4 January 1811. Richard COLLINS and Polly Carter. Sur. William Carter. p 473

25 November 1807. Thomas COLLINS and Catherine Loggins, dau. Martin Loggins who is surety. p 403

12 November 1785. George COMBS and Frances Nance, dau. William Nance who is surety. Married 21 November by Rev. John Williams. p 78

18 June 1800. William COMBS and Michael Traylor. Sur. Thomas Blanks. See William Coombs. p 291

23 November 1797. William G. CONNOLLY and Polly Davis. Married by Rev. Edward Almond. Ministers' Returns p 22

24 December 1779. Benjamin COOK and Catharine Brewer, dau. Sackville Brewer. Sur. William Cook. p 34

29 December 1791. David COOK and Martha Brewer, dau. Sackville Brewer. Sur. Benjamin Cook. Married same day by Rev. Henry Lester. p 168

4 November 1788. Henry COOK and Philby Cheatham, sister of William Cheatham. Sur. Henry Pamplin. Married 6 November by Rev. Thomas Johnston, who says Phebe. p 113

1 October 1798. Stephen COOK and Martha White Cook. Sur. James Brent. Stephen son of John Cook. p 273

26 December 1780. William COOK and Ann Baker, dau. Martin Baker. Sur. S. Brewer. p 39

5 November 1810. William COOK and Betsey Hundley. Sur. Warner Lewis. Married 14 November by Rev. Richard Dabbs. p 458

29 December 1807. Abraham COOKE and Nancy Richardson, dau. John Richardson. Sur. William Richardson. Married 31 December by Rev. John Fore. p 400

22 June 1800. William COOMBS and Michael Taylor. Married by Rev. Edward Almond. See William Combs. Ministers' Returns p 25

2 January 1804. John COOPER and Jincey Maddox, ward of Joseph Reynolds who is surety. John son of William Cooper. Married same day by Rev. John Chappell. p 362

18 May 1804. Philip COPELAND and Polly Evans, dau. Nancy Evans. Sur. Richard North. Married 21 May by Rev. Joshua Worley. p 358

15 January 1798. William COPELAND and Mary Anion. Sur. Peter Mason. Married 16 January by Rev. John Fore who says Polly Anyon. p 267

25 December 1793. Martin COVINGTON and Suckey Woodall, dau. Sampson
Woodall. Sur. William Woodall. Married 26 December by Rev. John
Weatherford. p 205

2 November 1768. Bartels COX and Mary Bouldin, dau. Thomas Bouldin.
Sur. Clement Read. p 7

26 February 1790. Benjamin COX and Susannah North, dau. Thomas North,
Jr. Sur. William Smith. See Benjamin Cocke. p 143

5 April 1773. Henry COX and Anne Madison. Sur. Roger Madison. p 18

4 November 1782. Jesse COX and Elizabeth Farley. Sur. James Watkins.
Jesse Cox from Mecklenburg County, son of John Cox. Married
19 November by Rev. Thomas Johnston. p 49

1 September 1783. Thomas COX and Rebecca Johnston, dau. Thomas Johnston.
Sur. Will Bouldin. Married 7 October by Rev. Thomas Johnston. p 57

24 July 1792. William COX and Sally Stembridge. Sur. Herod Reese.
Married same day by Rev. Obadiah Edge. p 170

13 November 1785. William COZENS and Hannah Jackson. Sur. Joseph Haily.
Married 19 November by Rev. Thomas Johnston. p 78

25 December 1766. John CRAFTON and Elizabeth Foster. John son of James
Crafton who consents. Wit. Richard and William Crafton. Sur. James
Foster. p 3

25 November 1783. William CRAIGHEAD and Sarah Wimbish (widow). Sur.
Jacob Morton. William Craighead of Lunenburg County. Married 5
December by Rev. John B. Smith. p 58

15 November 1803. William CRAWLEY and Sarah Davis, dau. James Davis.
Sur. Jacob Edwards. Married 17 November by Rev. William Spencer. p 343

7 February 1785. Daniel CREASY and Betty Hutcherson. Married by Rev.
John Weatherford. Above date when marriage was returned to Clerk's
Office. Ministers' Returns p 3

12 February 1797. Charles CRENSHAW and Martha Crenshaw. Sur. Cain
Jackson. Married 16 February by Rev. John Chappell. p 248

15 May 1780. Charles CRENSHAW and Martha Bedford, dau. Thomas Bedford.
Sur. Robert Bedford. p 37

16 September 1799. Cornelius CRENSHAW and Sarah Lee, dau. John Lee who
is surety. p 286

8 August 1795. David CRENSHAW and Susanna Barksdale, dau. W. Barksdale.
Sur. Richard Marshall. p 221

6 December 1788. Pleasant CRENSHAW and Patsey Jackson, dau. Elizabeth
Mitchell, ward of John Watson who is surety. Pleasant Crenshaw from
Lunenburg County. Married 18 December by Rev. William Mahon. p 114

15 December 1800. William CRENSHAW and Catherine Cheaney, dau. William
Cheaney, Sr. Sur. James Cheaney. Married 17 December by Rev.
Edward Almond. p 291

5 November 1792. Josiah CREWS and Peggy Jones. Sur. Zach Lawson. Married 15 November by Rev. Thomas Dobson. p 185

4 July 1803. William CREWS and Caty Jones. Sur. Nathan Buckley. Married 21 July by Rev. Thomas Dobson. p 348

13 November 1799. Robert CROUCH and Elizabeth Hundley, ward of Joel Watkins. Sur. John P. Hundley. Robert son of Richard Crouch. p 285

8 December 1813. Isaac CROWDER and Tabitha Hames Morgan, dau. John Morgan. Sur. William Phamp. Married 9 December by Rev. Richard Dabbs. p 505

6 December 1815. Miles T. CROWDER and Eliza Birthright, dau. Zachariah Birthright. Sur. David Shelton. Married 13 December by Rev. William Richards. p 523

25 July 1815. James CRUTCHER and Patsey Clements, orphan of Robert Clements, ward of Philip Cheaney who is surety. p 523

31 July 1815. Reuben CRUTCHER and Eliza McCargo, dau. Robert McCargo who is surety. p 523

21 October 1807. William CRUTCHER and Susanna Dupree, dau. William Dupree who is surety. William son of Reuben Crutcher. p 403

6 January 1806. Leonard CRYMES and Janet Moore, dau. Robert Moore who is surety. Married 23 January by Rev. Edward Almond who says Jennett. p 396

22 December 1804. Major CUMBIE and Margaret McMichael, dau. John McMichael. Major son of Thomas Cumbie who is surety. Married 26 December by Rev. John Chappell. p 357

3 January 1785. Andrew CUNNINGHAM and Isabel Hannah, dau. Jane Hannah. Sur. William Thorp. Married 6 January by Rev. Thomas Johnston. p 81

2 September 1793. Andrew CUNNINGHAM and Sally F. Hundley, dau. Anthony Hundley. Sur. William Morton. Married 5 September by Rev. Thomas Dobson who says Sally L. p 198

13 October 1765. James CUNNINGHAM and Sarah Wright, dau. Joseph Wright. Sur. Andrew Kincade. p 2

10 March 1789. James CUNNINGHAM and Judith Hannah, dau. George and Jeane Hannah. Sur. Andrew Hannah. James son of Joseph Cunningham. Married 12 March by Rev. William Mahon. p 137

3 September 1798. Joseph CUNNINGHAM and Jennie Hannah. Sur. Joel Watkins. p 267

12 December 1792. Wright CUNNINGHAM and Nancy Taylor, dau. James Taylor. Sur. Munford De Jarnette. Wright son of James and Sarah (Wright) Cunningham. p 169

21 April 1786. George DABBS and Sarah Mitchell, dau. John Mitchell. Sur. Joseph Dabbs. George son of Richard Dabbs. Married 27 April by Rev. Thomas Johnston. p 85

22 December 1783. Joseph DABBS and Judith Tankersley, dau. John Tankersley who is surety. Joseph son of Richard Dabbs. Married 23 December by Rev. Thomas Johnston. p 60

7 February 1803. Josiah DABBS, Jr. and Polly Hannah, ward of George Hannah. Sur. George Dabbs. p 342

11 January 1804. Richard DABBS, Sr. and Anne Hannah (widow). Sur. Joel Watkins. p 363

28 October 1789. William DABBS and Elizabeth Hatchett, dau. John Hatchett. Sur. Joseph Dabbs. Married 31 October by Rev. Edward Almond. p 130

5 October 1772. John DABNEY and Peggy Smith, dau. Charles Smith. Sur. William Flournoy. p 14

6 December 1810. Asa B. DANIEL and Polly McCraw, dau. William McCraw. Sur. Robert Morton. p 453

9 December 1772. John DANIEL and Elizabeth Morton, dau. Joseph Morton. Sur. Jacob Morton. John brother of James Daniel. p 17

1 October 1810. John DANIEL and Elizabeth Julia Spencer, dau. Gideon Spencer who is surety. p 461

3 February 1795. Martin DANIEL and Polly Mims, dau. Mary Mims. Sur. William Vaughan. Married 6 February by Rev. Edward Almond. p 230

5 October 1812. Samuel DANIEL and Martha Friend, dau. Joseph Friend, Sr. Sur. William H. Morton. p 486

6 December 1779. William DANIEL and Hannah Cunningham, dau. James Cunningham who is surety. p 33

6 April 1813. William F. DANIEL and Martha Moseley, dau. Hillery Moseley. Sur. Thomas Read. Married 7 April by Rev. William Richards who says "Patsey". p 503

7 November 1803. Ballard DAVENPORT and Mildred S. Scott, ward of George Booker. Sur. Richard Davenport. Married 7 December by Rev. Joshua Worley. p 341

30 November 1813. Jack S. DAVENPORT and Lucy K. Lewis, dau. Griffin Lewis. Sur. Edgecomb S. Lewis. Married 2 December by Rev. Joshua Worley. p 502

15 December 1794. Matthew DAVENPORT and Polly Johnson. Sur. James Johnston. Married 25 December by Rev. John Weatherford. p 211

1 January 1793. Presley DAVENPORT and Susanna Glover, dau. Robert Glover. Sur. Benjamin Marshall. Married 3 January by Rev. William Mahon. p 196

19 October 1811. Richard DAVENPORT and Rebecca Johnston (widow). Sur. Thomas Read. Married 30 October by Rev. William Richards. p 475

14 September 1810. William DAVENPORT and Nancy Raine, dau. Thomas Raine who is surety. Married 4 October by Rev. John Chappell. p 454

22 November 1813. John DAVIS and Anne Phillips, dau. Anthony Phillips. Sur. John Phillips. Married 24 November by Rev. Jesse Branch. p 503

16 April 1810. Samuel DAVIS and Susanna Cardwell, dau. Margaret A. Cardwell. Sur. James Traylor. p 454

18 February 1812. Samuel DAVIS and Phoebe Blanton. Sur. Samuel Brafford. Married 19 February by Rev. Joshua Worley. p 490

25 November 1801. Temple DAVIS and Margaret Fore. Married by Rev. John Fore. Ministers' Returns p 27

26 January 1801. William DAVIS and Hezekiah (?) Bartow. Married by Rev. Obadiah Edge. Ministers' Returns p 25

18 January 1812. William F. DAVIS and Peggy Russell. Sur. Thomas Russell. p 485

11 February 1793. Nelson Carter DAWSON and Lucy Goode, dau. Philip Goode, Jr. Sur. Richard Marshall. Returned to May 1793 Court by Rev. John Chappell. p 189

15 December 1810. Joseph De GRAFFENREID and Martha Ann Jameson, dau. Clement Jameson. Sur. Jesse Vest. p 461

2 April 1792. Samuel De JARNETTE and Milly Rice. Sur. William Rice. Married 5 April by Rev. Henry Lester. p 182

8 December 1783. Christley DENIARD and Catherine Huntsman, dau. Adam Huntsman who is surety. p 60

17 December 1798. John DENNIS and Martha Elliott. Sur. Clement R. Jameson. Married 20 December by Rev. John Chappell. p 268

27 July 1814. Thomas DENTON and Rhoda Cheatham, dau. Bernard Cheatham who is surety. p 517

6 March 1786. Daniel DIAL and Patsey Penticost, dau. William Penticost who is surety. p 85

17 July 1797. Peter DICKERSON and Lucy Fore, dau. Peter Fore. Sur. James Fore. Married 19 July by Rev. Joshua Worley. p 249

24 August 1802. Tarpley DICKERSON and Nancy Read Lambert, dau. Le Roy Lambert who is surety. p 328

19 February 1793. Christopher DIGGS and Judith Barnes, dau. James Barnes. Sur. Robert Moore. Married 28 March by Rev. John Williams. p 193

25 August 1793. Willis DIGGS and Mary Williams, dau. Henry Williams. Sur. John Diggs. See Willis Biggs. p 192

5 September 1783. Jamex DIXON and Jane Bryant, dau. John Bryant. Sur. John Simmons. Married 6 September by Rev. Thomas Johnston who says Jeane. p 53

23 July 1811. Pleasant DIXON and Sally Burras Inge, dau. James Inge who is surety. Married 25 July by Rev. Thomas E. Jeter. p 465

7 August 1797. Reuben DIXON and Amy Blankenship. Sur. William Pigg. p25

14 October 1802. Griffin DODD and Peggy Sullivant. Married by Rev. William Richards. Ministers' Returns p 28

6 February 1786. James DOTSON and Frances North (widow). Sur. James Lowe. p 93

5 August 1803. Joel DOWNEY and Polly Crawley, sister of William Crawley who is surety. Joel son of James Downey. p 342

25 February 1794. John DOWNEY and Susanna Morris. Sur. Joseph Morris. John son of James Downey. Married 27 February by Rev. Thomas Dobson. p 211

20 December 1789. Nelson W. DREWELL and Susannah Weekley. Married by Rev. John Weatherford. Ministers' Returns p 12

6 January 1807. Austin DUFFER and Elizabeth Rawlins (widow). Sur. Edmund Duffer. Married 7 January by Rev. Edward Almond. p 401

19 April 1810. Austin DUFFER and Nancy Gregory, dau. Joseph Gregory who is surety. p 454

24 December 1803. Edmund DUFFER and Polly Gayle, dau. Thomas Gayle. Sur. Robert Gayle. Married 25 December by Rev. Edward Almond. p 342

14 November 1804. John DUFFER and Eavy Burchett. John son of Edmund Duffer, Sr. who is surety. Married 15 November by Rev. Edward Almond. p 362

3 August 1812. Seaton DUFFER and Nancy Elam, dau. Jean Elam. Sur. Samuel Elam. Seaton son of Edmund Duffer. Married 7 August by Rev. William Richards who says Mary Elam. p 485

6 September 1800. Edmund DUNN and Lucretia Hundley, widow of Elisha Hundley. Sur. John Locke. Edmund son of Thomas Dunn. Married 9 September by Rev. Thomas Dobson. p 290

22 August 1797. Lewis DUNN and Rebecca Elam, dau. Edward Elam. Sur. John Elam. Married 24 August by Rev. Edward Almond. p 249

4 October 1783. Thomas DUNNING and Jenney (Jamey?) Clements. Married by Rev. Thomas Johnston. Ministers' Returns p 4

28 December 1813. William DUPREE, Jr. and Betty Portwood, dau. Thomas Portwood. Sur. Thomas Roberts. William, Jr. son of William Dupree, Sr. p 503

8 November 1793. John DUPUY and Mary Watkins, dau. Joel Watkins. Sur. James Dupuy. Married 31 December by Rev. John B. Smith. p 59

24 June 1815. Jonas EAGLES and Lucy Haley, dau. John Haley. Sur. Thomas Eagles. p 529

24 December 1812. Thomas EAGLES and Mary Haley, dau. Jack Haley. Sur. Michael Carter. p 484

1 April 1782. Edward EANES and Jane Sublett. Married by Rev. John Weatherford. Ministers' Returns p 3

3 May 1813. Henry EANES and Sarah Eanes, dau. Arthur Eanes who is surety. Married 5 May by Rev. John Chappell. p 501

4 April 1785. Arthur EANS and Eleanor Murray. Sur. Drury Kersey. Married same day by Rev. John Weatherford. p 68

26 September 1812. William EANS and Patsey Scates, ward of Joseph Oliver. Sur. John Eanes. p 484

19 December 1800. William EAST and Rhoda Clark, dau. Isaac Clark. Sur. Edward Clark. William East of Pittsylvania County, son of Thomas East. Married 6 January 1801 by Rev. John Chappell. p 290

7 January 1788. Richard EASTER and Mary Chisolm, dau. William and Mary Chisolm. Sur. Joseph Ferrell. Married 10 January by Rev. Edward Almond. p 113

28 February 1793. Obadiah EDGE and Elizabeth Elam, dau. Edward Elam. Sur. John Tarply. Married same day by Rev. Edward Almond. p 189

6 May 1799. William Bacon EDGE and Lucy Tarpley, ward of John Tarpley. Sur. Obadiah Edge. p 287

13 November 1800. John EDMONDSON and Sally Snead. Married by Rev. Edward Almond. See John Edmunds. Ministers' Returns p 26

25 March 1806. Edwin EDMUNDS and Mildred Morton, dau. William Morton. Sur. Henry A. Watkins. Married 27 March by Rev. John H. Rice. p 395

1 February 1808. Henry EDMUNDS and Martha W. Morton, dau. William Morton. Sur. Henry A. Watkins. Married 3 February by Rev. John H. Rice. p 413

3 November 1800. John EDMUNDS and Sally Snead, dau. John Snead who is surety. See John Edmondson. p 290

30 June 1802. Benjamin EDWARDS and Polly Jones, dau. Godfrey Jones, Jr. who is surety. Married 1 July by Rev. William Spencer. p 326

15 November 1811. Bernard EDWARDS and Martha Davenport, dau. Richard Davenport. Sur. Jack S. Davenport. Married 26 November by Rev. Joshua Worley. p 467

11 November 1784. John EDWARDS and Sarah Hyde. Married by Rev. Thomas Johnston. Ministers' Returns p 4

1 May 1772. Richard EDWARDS and Sarah Richardson (widow). Sur. Blassingham Harvey. p 15

7 February 1814. Anderson G. ELAM and Latisha Weatherford, dau. Samuel Weatherford. Sur. Samuel Weatherford, Jr. p 516

17 November 1813. Chandler ELAM and Tabitha Harris, dau. Sally Harris. Sur. Jacob Hudson. Married 18 November by Rev. George Petty. p 501

28 May 1810. Edward ELAM and Lettice Wallace (widow). Sur. Thomas Chaffin. Married 1 June by Rev. Richard Dabbs. p 455

29 October 1782. Solomon Harmon ELAM and Phoebe Osborne, dau. Reps. Osborne. p 51

23 January 1813. Harmon ELAM and Nancy Dupree, dau. William Dupree.
Sur. William Dupree, Jr. Married 28 January by Rev. William
Richards. p 501

23 February 1788. James ELAM and Betsy Sharp, dau. Mack Sharp. Sur.
Thompson Farley. Married same day by Rev. John Williams. p 113

1 February 1790. Joel ELAM and Mary Ann Easter. Sur. Hill Hudson.
Married 3 February by Rev. John Williams. p 143

1 October 1787. Martin ELAM and Judith Barnes, dau. Francis Barnes.
Sur. John Eubank. Married 25 October by Rev. John Williams. p 108

8 December 1807. Reps. J. ELAM and Mary Gregory, dau. Joseph Gregory.
Sur. D. S. Brown. p 401

21 May 1808. Robert ELAM and Polly Richardson, dau. John Richardson.
Sur. Richard Richardson. p 412

29 April 1809. Thomas ELAM and Catherine Kemp (widow). Sur. Price
Roach. Married same day by Rev. Joseph Jenkins. p 435

16 July 1787. Ephraim ELDER and Patsey Matthews. Married by Rev. John
Weatherford. Ministers' Returns p 8

1 July 1799. John ELDER and Anne Johns. Sur. Edmund F. Patrick. p 286

11 September 1809. Bowling ELDRIDGE and Mildred Gaines. Sur. Thomas
Eldridge. p 435

6 February 1787. John ELGIN and Elizabeth Bumpass. Married by Rev.
John Weatherford. Ministers' Returns p 8

20 January 1780. Martin ELLIOTT and Anne Finch, dau. Adam Finch. Sur.
Joseph Lee. p 40

7 August 1787. Richard ELLIOTT and Anne Jameson (widow of William
Jameson). Sur. Abner Nash. Married by Rev. John Williams. p 101

30 September 1793. Dr. Thomas C. ELLIOTT and Peggy Jameson, dau. Anne
Elliott. Sur. Robert Elliott. (Probably dau. William Jameson and
Anne Read. m. 9 Dec. 1768. She m. 2nd. 1787 Richard Elliott). Married
3 October by Rev. Henry Lester. p 205

5 August 1799. Ellison ELLIS and Priscilla Johnston, dau. Rev. Thomas
Johnston. Sur. Thomas Cox. Married 9 August by Rev. Edward Almond.
p 280

2 October 1797. Thomas ELLIS and Nancy White. Sur. John Foster. p 259

13 October 1801. William ELLIS and Mary Friend, dau. Joseph Friend.
Sur. George C. Friend. p 302

5 June 1786. James ELMORE and Polly Elam, dau. Edward Elam. Sur.
William Elmore. Married 8 June by Rev. Thomas Johnston. p 94

11 July 1786. James ELMORE and Jean Clements (widow). Sur. Thomas
Chaffin. Married same day by Rev. John Williams. p 89

15 October 1803. James ELMORE and Polly Hamlett (widow). Sur. William Green. p 330

4 July 1785. William ELMORE and Susanna Butler, dau. John Butler. Sur. James Tarpley. Married 20 July by Rev. Thomas Johnston. p 68

24 October 1792. Bartlett ESTES and Mary Blankenship, dau. John Blankenship. Sur. Richard Bouldin. Married 26 September (October?) by Rev. John Williams. p 172

8 November 1798. Robert ESTES and Mary Smith. Married by Rev. Edward Almond. Ministers' Returns p 23

5 January 1802. James EUBANKS and Clarkey Mays, dau. Richard Mays. Sur. Cornelius Crenshaw. Married 17 January by Rev. Edward Almond. p 326

25 January 1783. John EUBANKS and Sarah Hendrick dau. Gustavus Hendrick. Sur. Joseph Lee. Married 30 January by Rev. Thomas Johnston. p 56

1 August 1808. John EUBANKS and America Goode, dau. Philip Goode. Sur. Robert Williams. Married 4 August by Rev. Richard Dabbs, Jr. p 412

19 December 1783. David EUDALEY and Mary Ann Arnold. Married by Rev. Thomas Johnston. Ministers Returns p 2

13 October 1807. Elisha EUDALY and Peggy Elmore, dau. James Elmore. Sur. Jeremiah Featherstone. p 408

19 October 1810. James EUDALY and Polly Campbell, dau. Archibald and Margaret (Arnold) Campbell, grand-dau. James Arnold, Sr. Sur. Adam Loving. p 455

1 October 1787. John EUDALY and Mary Tarpley, dau. James Tarpley. Sur. Carless Featherstone. Married same day by Rev. Thomas Johnston. p 108

25 December 1811. William EUDALY and Polly Pollard. Sur. William Blanks. p 467

6 February 1794. William FALLIN and Elizabeth Hames. Married by Rev. Edward Almond. See William Fallis. Ministers' Returns p 18

3 February 1794. William FALLIS and Elizabeth Hames. Sur. William Hames. See William Fallin. p 212

1 April 1765. Elisha FARIS and Mary Vaughan, dau. Thomas Vaughan. Sur. John Vaughan. p 2

24 January 1799. John FARIS and Patsey Vaughter, sister of Lemuel Vaughter who is surety with Ludwell Vaughter. p 280

29 November 1789. Archer FARLEY and Ann Robertson, dau. Henry Robertson. Sur. Brooks Robertson. p 127

24 July 1811. James FARLEY and Elizabeth Davis, dau. Asa Davis. Sur. Gressett Green. Married 25 July by Rev. John Campbell. p 467

21 June 1803. Anderson FARMER and Betsy Smith Lambert, dau. Le Roy Lambert who is surety. p 338

26 August 1794. Hezekiah FEATHERSTON and Nancy Tarpley, dau. John Tarpley. Sur. Charles Featherston. Married 28 August by Rev. Edward Almond. p 212

21 November 1782. Carlus FEATHERSTONE and Gilley Brumfield. Married by Rev. Thomas Johnston. Ministers' Returns p 1

10 December 1787. Charles FEATHERSTONE and Lucy Elmore, dau. James Elmore. Sur. James Tarpley. Married 12 December by Rev. Thomas Johnston. p 107

20 January 1815. James FEATHERSTONE and Betsy Elmore, dau. James Elmore. Sur. William Featherstone. p 534

4 January 1796. Jeremiah FEATHERSTONE and Elizabeth Elmore, dau. James Elmore. Sur. Jesse Elmore. p 234

18 January 1814. Jeremiah FEATHERSTONE and Anne Green, dau. Benjamin Green. Sur. Paschall Wingo. Married same day by Rev. William Fears. p 516

4 January 1809. Robert FEATHERSTONE and Martha Russell, dau. John Russell. Sur. Hezekiah Russell. p 435

18 December 1813. William FEATHERSTONE and Sally Vaughan, dau. William Vaughan. Sur. Snelling Vaughan. p 502

18 May 1804. Wyley FEATHERSTONE and Sally Elmore. Sur. Samuel Green. Wyley son of Jeremiah Featherstone. p 365

17 April 1805. John FENNELL and Peggy Bedford, dau. Thomas Bedford, deceased. Sur. Ephraim Bouldin. Married same day by Rev. Mathew Dance. p 374

7 April 1788. Joel FERGUSON and Usley (Ursula) Sublett, dau. Benjamin Sublett. Sur. Matthew Jordan. Married same day by Rev. Joshua Worley. p 115

3 November 1783. Joseph FERRELL and Elizabeth Chisolm, dau. William Chisolm. Sur. William St. John. p 58

4 January 1809. Bannister FERRILL and Jinsey Collins, dau. Joel Collins who is surety. Married 5 January by Rev. David McCargo. p 436

5 August 1800. Thomas FINCH and Susanna Haskins (widow). Sur. Hillery Moseley. Married 25 September by Rev. Edward Almond. p 289

25 November 1815. William FINCH and Sarah Moore. Sur. Richard Moore. Married same day by Rev. James Robertson. p 533

4 November 1793. Zachariah FINCH and Polly Bacon. Sur. Langston Bacon. Zachariah son of Adam Finch. Married 14 November by Rev. John Williams who says Mary Bacon. p 200

10 October 1803. David FLOURNOY and Mary Morton, dau. Jacob Morton. Sur. William D. Morton. p 338

15 December 1787. William FLOYD and Elizabeth Farguson, dau. Thomas Farguson. Sur. William Johnson. Married 18 December by Rev. Joshua Worley. p 106

3 September 1804. William FLOYD and Prudence Farguson. Sur. William Raine. p 365

27 December 1810. Dr. Charles D. FONTAINE and Nancy Carrington, dau. Paul Carrington, Jr. Sur. Edward Carrington. Married same day by Rev. John H. Rice who says Anne. p 455

16 December 1787. Ezekiah FORD and Anne Garnett, dau. James Garnett. Sur. Charles McKinney. Married 21 December by Rev. John Weatherford who says Anne Garret. p 106

23 April 1791. John FORD and Frances Hanes, dau. John Hanes. Sur. Richard Brizendine. Married 25 April by Rev. John Williams. p 155

5 January 1798. John FORD and Elizabeth Brizendine, dau. Isaac Brizendine. Sur. Josiah Stokes. Married 6 January by Rev. Edward Almond. p 272

26 December 1793. Thomas FORD and Rebecca Burton, dau. Thomas Burton. Sur. John Ashworth. Thomas son of John Ford. Married 2 January 1794 by Rev. John Williams. p 199

26 December 1793. William FORD and Dicey Vaughan, widow of Ligon Vaughan. Sur. John Ainsworth. Married 4 January 1794 by Rev. Edward Almond. p 200

15 June 1790. James FORE and Elizabeth Jordan. Sur. Matthew Jordan. James son of Peter Fore. Married same day by Rev. Joshua Worley. p 154

26 May 1785. George FORE and Elizabeth Jordan. Married by Rev. John Weatherford. Ministers' Returns p 4

27 March 1782. John FORE and Sarah Sublett. Married by Rev. John Weatherford. Ministers' Returns p 2

18 March 1793. John FORE and Marjory Maloyd. Sur. Andrew Wallace. Married 19 March by Rev. William Mahon. p 199

7 January 1799. John FORE and Anne Fore, dau. Peter Fore. Sur. James Fore. Married same day by Rev. Joshua Worley. p 280

6 June 1803. John FORE and Susanna Farrow, dau. Charles Farrow. Sur. James More. Married 9 June by Rev. Obadiah Edge. p 337

12 October 1785. Philip FORE and Nance Heaton, widow of John Heaton. Sur. Joseph Whorley. p 69

7 July 1788. James FOSTER and Elizabeth Haney, dau. John Haney. Sur. Josiah Foster. Married 10 July by Rev. Thomas Johnston. p 115

15 October 1792. James Johnson FOSTER and Elizabeth Hayze, dau. John Hayze. Sur. Joshua Foster. p 176

5 September 1785. George FOSTER and Sally Wilkes, dau. Benjamin Wilkes who is surety. Married 29 September by Rev. Thomas Johnston. p 69

21 December 1791. George FOSTER and Sally Hankins. Sur. John Hankins. Married 22 December by Rev. Drury Lacy. p 158

22 December 1802. George Watts FOSTER and Betsey Bass Hatchett, dau. Thomas Hatchett who is surety. p 326

15 August 1801. John FOSTER and Phoebe Hatchett, dau. Thomas Hatchett who is surety. p 313

28 December 1808. John FOSTER and Petty Foster, ward of William Foster who is surety. Married 3 January 1809 by Rev. Richard Dabbs. p 427

6 January 1782. Joshua FOSTER and Mary Foster, dau. Josiah Foster. Sur. Robert Bowman. p 48

1 October 1798. Josiah FOSTER, Jr. and Elizabeth Webb. Sur. Josiah Foster, Sr. Married 4 October by Rev. William Richards. p 268

3 August 1804. Misheak FOSTER and Nettie Taylor, dau. Francis Taylor. Sur. Zenas Foster. p 365

28 August 1804. Richard FOSTER and Betsey Mann Foster, dau. George Foster. Sur. William Foster. Married 30 August by Rev. Richard Dabbs, Jr. p 366

14 January 1791. Samuel FOSTER and Elizabeth Breedlove, dau. John Breedlove. Sur. William Breedlove. Married by Rev. John B. Smith. p 162

3 October 1803. Singleton FOSTER and Sally Terry, ward of Richard Dabbs, Jr. Singleton son of Josiah Foster who is surety. p 338

5 November 1810. William FOSTER and Polly Rice, dau. William Rice. Sur. Ralph Jackson. p 459

5 January 1797. Zenas FOSTER and Dinah Taylor, dau. Frances Taylor. Sur. John Foster. p 259

14 September 1790. John FOWLER and Anne Almond. Married by Rev. Edward Almond. Ministers' Returns p 12

13 October 1796. Archibald FOWLKES and Letty Rawlins. Married by Rev. Edward Almond. See Archibald Fulks. Ministers' Returns p 20

6 January 1806. Elijah FOWLKES and Elizabeth Sullivant, ward of John McCargo who is surety. Married 14 January by Rev. Edward Almond. p 397

3 February 1801. Mordecai FOWLKES and Mary Allday, dau. Perrin Allday. Sur. Thomas Harvey. p 306

22 October 1801. Nathaniel FOWLKES and Ann Osborne Barnes, dau. Francis Barnes. Sur. Gabriel Fowlkes. Married 26 October by Rev. William Richards. p 313

9 June 1803. Edmund FRANKLIN and Elizabeth Cook. Married by Rev. John Chappell. See Edward Franklin. Ministers' Returns p 29

6 June 1803. Edward FRANKLIN and Elizabeth Cook, dau. Thomas Cook who is surety. See Edmund Franklin. p 339

22 December 1794. John FRANKLIN and Polly Davenport. Sur. Richard Davenport. Married 25 December by Rev. William Mahon. p 212

7 May 1792. Joseph FRANKLIN and Susanna Mullins. Sur. William A. Sublett. p 186

27 January 1792. Hugh FRAZIER and Anne Morton, dau. John Morton. Sur. Jacob Morton. Married 1 February by Rev. Drury Lacy. p 172

10 April 1804. George C. FRIEND and Martha M. Moon, dau. Archelious Moon. Sur. William L. Morton. p 366

28 November 1808. Joseph FRIEND and Julia Elliott, dau. Nancy Elliott. Sur. Clement P. Jameson. p 412

15 May 1815. Thomas FRIEND and Mary C. Gaines, dau. Williams Gaines. Sur. Joseph Wyatt. p 534

5 February 1796. Archibald FULKS and Letty Rolings, dau. John Rolings who is surety. See Archibald Fowlkes. p 235

1 March 1809. Asa FULKS and Rhody Bottom, dau. Miles Bottom. Sur. Daniel Fulks. Married 2 March by Rev. Richard Dabbs. p 436

2 August 1768. Joseph FUQUA and Elizabeth Bedford, dau. Thomas Bedford. Sur. Stephen Bedford. p 7

30 June 1779. Joseph FUQUA, Jr. and Catharine Palmer, dau. John and Mary Palmer. Sur. Richard Booker. p 35

18 March 1783. Joseph FUQUA and Mary Burge, dau. Drury Burge. Sur. James Baker. Married 20 March by Rev. Thomas Johnston. p 54

25 February 1812. Capt. Nathaniel William FUQUA and Susanna Daniel. Sur. William P. Daniel. p 485

1 April 1771. Samuel FUQUA and Hannah Bates. Sur. Joseph Bates. p 12

- April 1797. Samuel FUQUA and Polly Armistead. Married by Rev. Archibald Alexander. Ministers' Returns p 21

17 December 1807. Seth FUQUA and Eliza Ann Ford. Sur. Samuel Fuqua. Married 24 December by Rev. Richard Dabbs, Jr. p 400

13 May 1797. William FUQUA and Elizabeth Barnes, dau. Sarah Barnes. Sur. Henry Barnes (brother). Married 20 May by Rev. John Chappell. p 259

22 March 1806. Edmund GAINES and Sally Jackson, dau. Cain Jackson. Sur. William Edwards. Married 27 March by Rev. John H. Rice. p 394

1 March 1773. Richard GAINES and Margaret Cunningham, dau. James Cunningham who is surety. p 19

16 October 1802. Richard GAINES, Jr. and Amy C. Green, dau. John Green. Sur. Horatio Gates Brewer. Married same day by Rev. John Chappell. p 327

26 December 1805. Richard GAINES and Elizabeth Daniel, dau. William Pride Daniel. Sur. Samuel Daniel. Married 2 January 1806, by Rev. Jesse Lee. p 375

6 January 1812. Richard W. GAINES and Nancy B. Morton, dau. Jacob
Morton. Sur. Robert Morton. p 483

16 April 1783. Thomas GAINES and Sarah White, dau. John White. Sur.
Daniel White. Married 17 April by Rev. Thomas Johnston. p 56

24 September 1811. Thomas GAINES and Elizabeth Jackson, dau. Cain
Jackson. Sur. Benjamin Moseley. p 466

16 September 1794. William GAINES and Mary Latene Jennings, dau. Robert
Jennings. Sur. Jack Smith Davenport. Married by Rev. John Chappell.
Returned to February Court 1795. p 213

18 March 1806. William GAINES and Elizabeth Carter. Sur. Claiborne
Barksdale. Married 20 March by Rev. John H. Rice. p 395

29 February 1803. Joshua GALIMORE and Betsey Flood, dau. William Flood
who is surety. p 333

9 May 1813. George GALLIMORE and Patsey Flood. Sur. John Flood.
Married 10 May by Rev. Richard Dabbs. p 499

1 October 1805. David GARLAND and Martha Sublett, dau. Benjamin Sublett.
Sur. Matthew Sublett. Married 5 October by Rev. Joshua Worley. p 375

1 January 1787. William GEORGE and Elizabeth Jackson, dau. Lewis Jackson who is surety. Married by Rev. Thomas Johnston who says 4 July.
p 103

12 December 1792. Mitchell GILL and Nancy Dabbs. Sur. George Dabbs.
p 183

7 July 1794. Allen GILLIAM and Martha Cox Barnes, dau. Francis Barnes,
Sr. Sur. Stephen Hay. Married 8 July by Rev. John Williams. p 213

2 February 1813. Charles GILLIAM and Patsey Wyatt, dau. John Wyatt who
is surety. p 499

18 April 1808. John GILLIAM and Nancy Brown, ward of James Brown who
is surety. p 418

3 April 1813. John GILLIAM and Margaret Tankersley, dau. John Tankersley. Sur. Archibald Haley. Married 5 April by Rev. William Fears.
p 499

24 December 1786. Robert GILLIAM and Priscilla Mosbey, dau. Allison
Mosbey. Robert son of James Gilliam. Sur. James Johnson. Married
by Rev. Thomas Johnston who says 26 October. p 83

3 February 1800. Thomas GILLIAM and Sally B. Pettus. Married by Rev.
Edward Almond. Ministers' Returns p 25

17 July 1800. William GILLIAM and Elizabeth D. Pettus. Married by Rev.
Edward Almond. Ministers' Returns p 26

3 November 1785. Bartholomew GIVIN and Susanna Bly Mullins, dau. David
Mullins who is surety. Married 4 November by Rev. Thomas Johnston.
p 69

16 September 1808. William GLASS and Sally Davis, dau. Samuel Davis
who is surety. Married same day by Rev. Bernard Todd. p 149

4 December 1815. Charles GLINN and Polly W. Hancock, dau. John Hancock
who is surety. p 533

20 November 1781. Isaac GOARE and Sarah Traynum. Sur. William Traynum.
p 45

24 September 1774. William GOARE, Jr. and Mary - . Sur. Samuel Comer.
p 22

4 November 1805. Hillery GOODE and Sarah Bacon, dau. Langston Bacon.
Sur. John G. Bacon. Hillery son of Mackerness Goode. Married same
day by Rev. Thomas Hardie. p 375

24 October 1815. John GOODE and Margaret Miller, dau. James Miller.
Sur. John C. Miller. p 534

15 October 1770. Mackness GOODE, Jr. and Mary Moseley. Sur. John
Osborne. p 9

7 November 1808. Thomas GOODE and Mary Rebecca Barksdale, dau. Claiborne Barksdale. Sur. William Bacon. p 420

8 May 1787. Joseph GRAMMER and Elizabeth Pryor. Sur. Jacob Huntsman.
Married 10 June by Rev. John Weatherford. p 99

4 June 1787. Joseph GRAMMER and Elizabeth Pryor. Sur. Adam Huntsman.
(Evidently same as above.) p 99

19 October 1810. Asa GREEN and Mary Eudaley, dau. David Eudaley.
Sur. Adam Loving. p 448

4 December 1787. Benjamin GREEN and Cary Arnold. Married by Rev.
Thomas Johnston. Ministers' Returns p 9

17 July 1804. Davis GREEN and Ann Towler, dau. Joseph and Elizabeth
Towler. Sur. Luke Towler. p 351

30 November 1813. Epps GREEN and Margaret Arnold, dau. James Arnold, Jr.
Sur. Thomas Arnold. p 500

21 August 1797. Fortunatus GREEN and Martha Mullins, dau. Elizabeth
Mullins. Sur. William Roach. Fortunatus son of Malachi Green.
Married 22 August by Rev. Joshua Worley. p 250

30 November 1807. James GREEN and Betsey Eudaly, dau. Moses Eudaly
who is surety. p 437

14 August 1794. John GREEN and Levice Kennady. Sur. Reuben Herndon.
p 213

19 September 1796. Liberty GREEN and Peggy Brent. Sur. Parish Green.
Liberty son of Thomas Green. Married 28 September by Rev. John
Chappell. p 235

7 March 1803. Samuel GREEN and Nancy ELMORE, sister of James Elmore
who is surety. p 333

23 December 1801. William GREEN and Winny Elmore, dau. James Elmore
who is surety. p 314

4 November 1805. William GREEN and Nancy Nance, dau. Hood Nance who
is surety. Married 13 November by Rev. James Elmore. p 372

13 October 1785. Bartley GREENWOOD and Mary Sublett. Married by Rev.
John Weatherford. Ministers' Returns p 5

4 February 1793. John GREGORY and Elizabeth Neal, dau. Thomas Neal.
Sur. Thomas Chaffin. p 198

6 January 1807. Joseph GREGORY and Mary Magdalen Herndon (widow). Sur.
Austin Duffer. Married 8 January by Rev. Edward Almond. p 408

22 November 1813. Thomas S. GREGORY and Polly A. Barnes, dau. Francis
Barnes, Jr. Sur. Cornelius Barnes. Married 25 November by Rev.
William Richards. p 500

9 April 1814. Thomas GREGORY and Ednea J. Elam, dau. Soloman H. Elam.
Sur. Harmon Elam. p 519

7 February 1785. James GRIFFIN and Delpha Adkins. Above date when
married was returned to Clerk's Office. Ministers' Returns p 3

3 September 1797. William GRIFFIN and Peggy Almond, dau. Elisha
Almond who is surety. p 254

8 December 1767. James GRIGG and Mary White, dau. John White who is
surety. p 4

14 May 1784. - GWIN and Neuraney (?) Mullins. Married by Rev. John
Weatherford. Ministers' Returns p 3

6 August 1787. William GWINN and Agness Mullins, dau. David Mullins.
Sur. Nicholas Bowers. William son of Bartlett Gwinn. Married
7 August by Rev. Thomas Johnston. p 99

12 February 1791. John HADEN and Susanna Roach, dau. John Roach, Sr.
Sur. James Roach. p 161

7 December 1801. Berryman HAILEY and Nancy Dunn, dau. William Dunn.
Sur. Obadiah Hendrick. Married 17 December by Rev. Edward Almond.
p 302

14 February 1805. Thomas HAILEY and Jane Bradberry. Sur. Thomas
Hayes. Married same day by Rev. Thomas Hardie. p 376

13 December 1790. Acquilla HAILY and Sarah Galimore, dau. William
Galimore. Sur. Thomas Hayes. See Aquilla Haley. p 152

13 September 1790. Benjamin HAILY and Elizabeth Williams. Sur. Robert Williams. See Benjamin Haley. p 142

7 February 1785. Joseph HAILY and Elizabeth Collins, dau. Richard Collins. Sur. Thomas Hatchett. p 70

16 December 1790. Aquilla HALEY and Sarah Gallimore. Married by Rev. Edward Almond. See Acquilla Haily. Ministers' Returns p 12

23 February 1806. Archibald HALEY and Judith Haley, dau. John Haley. Sur. Thomas Hendrick. p 394

14 September 1790. Benjamin HALEY and Elizabeth Williams. Married by Rev. Edward Almond. See Benjamin Haily. Ministers' Returns p 12

8 November 1793. Benjamin HALEY and Patsey Grews, dau. Richard Crews, Sur. Thomas Thorp. Married 12 November by Rev. Thomas Dobson. p 195

25 January 1803. Benjamin HALEY and Josie Wells. Sur. Martin Worthy. Married same day by Rev. Edward Almond who says Joice Wells. p 332

22 September 1798. Charles HALEY and Polly Walker, dau. Daniel Walker who is surety. Married 25 September by Rev. John Chappell. p 270

19 August 1797. Humphrey HALEY and Lucy Hammons. Sur. John Roberts. Married 31 August by Rev. Edward Almond. p 251

2 June 1809. Joseph HALEY and Mary May, widow of David May. Sur. Archibald Haley. p 442

20 November 1789. Pleasant HALEY and Sarah Collings, dau. Mary Collings. Sur. James Mullings. Married 26 November by Rev. Thomas Johnston. p 127

4 August 1794. Robert HALEY and Peggy Mullings. Sur. William Mullings. Robert son of Thomas Haley. p 214

6 August 1804. Spencer HALEY and Nancy Weatherford, dau. James Weatherford. Sur. James Inge. Married same day by Rev. Richard Dabbs. p 353

9 November 1811. Wyatt HALEY and Nancy S. Hightower. Sur. Woodward Haley. p 472

19 February 1793. John HALL and Sally Barnes, dau. James Barnes. Sur. Robert Moore. Married 21 February by Rev. John Williams. p 202

4 March 1799. William HALL and Martha Bibb. Sur. Francis Gaines. Married 14 March by Rev. John Chappell. p 281

1 March 1790. James HAMBLETON and Patsey Rowton, dau. William Rowton who is surety. Married 8 March by Rev. Archibald McRobert. p 153

4 February 1793. James HAMBLETON and Patsey Ware McCraw. Sur. Stephen McCraw. See James Hamilton. p 196

11 November 1772. James HAMBLETT and Mary Bedford, dau. Thomas Bedford. p 16

22 December 1806. Coleman HAMBLIN and Ritta Williamson, dau. Jacob Williamson. Sur. Richard Rutledge. Married by Rev. David McCargo. p 394

28 December 1804. Francis HAMBLIN and Milly Ashworth. Sur. Jonathan Ashworth. See Thomas Hamblin. p 354

30 December 1804. Thomas HAMBLIN and Milly Ashworth. Married by Rev. Edward Almond. See Francis Hamblin. Ministers' Returns p 32

12 October 1808. Edmund HAMES and Sarah C. Garrett, dau. Francis Garrett. Sur. William Hames. p 424

21 February 1793. James HAMILTON and Betsey McCraw. Married by Rev. William Mahon. See James Hambleton. Ministers' Returns p 16

2 November 1813. Rowton HAMILTON and Jinsey Jackson, dau. Thomas Jackson. Sur. Thomas Grymes. p 500

4 April 1808. James HAMLETT and Nancy P. White, dau. William White who is surety. Married 21 April by Rev. Richard Dabbs, Jr. p 425

6 January 1812. James HAMLETT and Elizabeth Robey, dau. Eli Robey who is surety. p 483

5 September 1808. George HAMLETT and Lucy Mitchell. Sur. William Dabbs. Married 8 September by Rev. Richard Dabbs. p 425

11 March 1775. William HAMLETT and Rebecca Bedford, dau. Stephen Bedford. Sur. John Collier. William son of James Hamlett. p 27

6 June 1785. William HAMLETT and Catherine Collins, dau. Mary Collins. Sur. John Collier. Married 16 June by Rev. Thomas Johnston. p 70

12 October 1811. William HAMLETT and Nancy Armistead, dau. William Armistead. Sur. John Armistead. p 472

1 December 1794. Edward HAMLIN and Nancy Brook. Sur. Joel Brook. Married 24 December by Rev. Edward Almond. p 214

5 February 1798. Thomas HAMMOCK and Katey Hazelwood. Sur. William Hazelwood. Thomas son of Lewis Hammock. Married 8 February by Rev. Obadiah Edge. p 269

11 April 1815. Clifton G. HAMNER and Sarah Anderson, dau. Charles Anderson. Sur. James T. Wheeler. Clifton son of Morris Hamner. Married 13 April by Rev. John Chappell. p 533

20 January 1915. Morris HAMNER and Lucy Featherstone Morton (widow). Sur. Samuel Hamner. Married 31 January by Rev. John McLean. p 531

5 November 1787. Douglas HANCOCK and Molly Harvey, dau. Thomas Harvey who is surety. Married 12 November by Rev. John Weatherford. p 98

1 December 1794. John HANCOCK and Frances Warren Brown. Sur. James
Brown. Married by Rev. John Chappell. Returned to February Court
1795. p 214

1 September 1790. Martin HANCOCK and Sally Harvey. Sur. Thomas Harvey.
p 147

1 October 1792. Thomas HANCOCK and Vina Cheatham. Sur. Samuel Pryor.
Benjamin Cook consents. Returned to January Court 1793 by Rev. John
Chappell. p 179

29 September 1791. Isaac HANEY and Susanna Terry, dau. George Terry,
Sr. Sur. James Haney. p 159

19 April 1785. James HANEY and Frances Ann Foster, dau. Mary Buckner,
sister of John Foster. Sur. Josiah Foster. Married 21 April by
Rev. Thomas Johnston. p 70

27 July 1782. John HANEY and Elizabeth Read. Married by Rev. John
Weatherford. Ministers' Returns p 2

January Court. 1793. Hathan HANEY and Mary Williamson. Married by
Rev. John Chappell. Returned January Court. See Nathan Havery.
Ministers' Returns p 13

4 June 1789. Thomas HANEY and Nancy Buckner. Married by Rev. Thomas
Johnston. Ministers' Returns p 10

2 December 1785. William HANEY and Nancy Terry, dau. George Terry.
Sur. Lewis Gaines. Married by Rev. Thomas Johnston who says
24 November. p 73

6 July 1799. Daniel HANKINS and Lina Toombs, dau. William Toombs who
is surety. p 281

18 March 1792. John HANKINS and Fellisha Collins, dau. Mary Collins.
Sur. James Mullins. Married 22 March by Rev. John Williams. p 186

5 November 1804. Robert HANKINS and Polly Foster, dau. John Foster.
Sur. Daniel Hankins. p 352

4 November 1805. George HANNAH and Patsey Brent, dau. James Brent.
Sur. John Patrick. Married 7 November by Rev. John H. Rice. p 377

19 July 1791. John HANNAH and Elizabeth Motley, dau. Joel Motley.
Sur. George Hundley. p 165

5 July 1782. Robert HANNAH and Rebeccah Spencer. Married by Rev. John
Weatherford. Ministers' Returns p 2

13 December 1790. William HANNAH and Milley Berkeley, dau. Alexander
Berkeley. Sur. Robert Hannah. p 139

30 July 1793. Matthew HARBARD and Polly Adkins, dau. Joseph Adkins.
Sur. James Thomson. Matthew son of John Harbard. See Mathew
Harbert. p 196

1 August 1793. Mathew HARBERT and Polly W. Atkins. Married by Rev. Henry Lester. See Matthew Harbard. Ministers' Returns p 17

7 June 1802. Edmund HARD and Polly Whitlow, dau. Dabney Whitlow. Sur. Hillary Moseley. See Edmund Hoard. p 328

17 November 1797. David HAREFIELD and Peggy Haskins. Sur. Josiah Foster. Indexed Hatfield - See David Hatfield. p 251

7 January 1803. John HARMAN and Milly Roach, dau. John Roach who is surety. p 336

26 December 1782. James HARPER and Agness Weatherford. Married by Rev. John Weatherford. Ministers' Returns p 3

22 November 1805. John HARRALD and Nancy Davis, dau. Temple Davis. Sur. Josiah Farrow. Married 26 November by Rev. John Fore. p 377

18 December 1789. Claiborn HARRIS and Salley Hudson, dau. Daniel Hudson. Sur. Hill Hudson. p 134

23 June 1808. James HARRIS and Nancy Belcher, widow of Thomas Belcher. Sur. Levy Brooks. Married 24 June by Rev. George Petty. p 424

17 December 1782. John HARRIS and Mary Baugh. Sur. James Brent. Married 25 December by Rev. Drury Lacy. p 181

17 March 1789. John HARRIS and Elizabeth Overstreet, dau. William Overstreet. Sur. Edward Day. Married 30 March by Rev. John Weatherford. p 132

10 February 1812. John HARRIS and Nancy Alderson, dau. John Alderson. Sur. George Dabbs. Married 20 February by Rev. Richard Dabbs. p 484

17 October 1792. Joseph HARRIS and Joanna Almond. Sur. Thomas Read. Married 18 October by Rev. Joshua Worley. p 169

6 June 1803. Robert HARRIS and Polly Bailey, dau. Mary Bailey. Sur. Carloss Wood. p 332

16 November 1791. Samuel HARRIS and Nancy Overton, dau. William Overton. Sur. Thomas Moore. Married 1 December by Rev. Thomas Dobson. p 161

15 May 1809. Thomas HARRIS and Anne L. Cobb. Sur. William H. Britton. Married same day by Rev. Robert Hurt. p 438

4 September 1780. Thompson HARRIS and Frankey Davidson, dau. Ambrose Davidson. Sur. Robert McCune. p 40

2 December 1809. William HARRIS and Tempy Monday, dau. William and Nancy Monday. Sur. Levi Brooks. Married same day by Rev. George Petty. p 437

7 August 1811. William HARRIS and Patsey Patrick, dau. Edmund Patrick who is surety. p 466

5 January 1796. Andrew HARRISON and Mildred Read. Married by Rev. Arnold Alexander. Ministers' Returns p 20

2 January 1786. Charles HARRISON and Nancy Rawlins, dau. Peter Rawlins. Sur. Smith Milner. Married by Rev. John Weatherford who says 29 December 1785. p 95

5 February 1813. Charles HARROWAY and Elizabeth Minton, dau. Simon Minton who is surety. p 509

25 November 1784. Beasley HART and Betty Winn, dau. John Winn. Sur. Robert Belcher. Married 28 November by Rev. Thomas Johnston. p 64

23 December 1801. Charles HART and Peggy Reynolds, dau. William Reynolds. Sur. Reuben Hart. p 301

11 December 1811. Coleman HART and Betsey Morgan, dau. Robert Morgan who is surety. p 471

27 September 1783. Cornelius HART and Edy Hart, dau. (step-dau?) Josephus Perrin who is surety. Cornelius son of John Hart, Sr. p 53

29 September 1783. Cornelius HART and Edy Perrin. Married by Rev. Thomas Johnston. She must have been Edy Perrin, dau. of Josephus Perrin. Ministers' Returns p 3

26 January 1798. Reuben HART and Martha Haskins Hart. Sur. William Hart. Married 31 January by Rev. Edward Almond. p 269

25 November 1801. Reuben HART and Polly Williams, dau. William Williams who is surety. Married 3 December by Rev. Thomas Dobson. p 302

26 January 1798. Thomas HART and Leanah Dickerson. Sur. William Hames. Married 31 January by Rev. Edward Almond. p 268

16 January 1801. William HART and Betsey Reynolds, dau. William Reynolds. Sur. Beasley Hart. Married 28 January by Rev. John Chappell. p 314

6 January 1796. Isham HARVEY and Drucilla Harvey. Sur. Thomas Harvey. p 235

4 September 1812. Isham HARVEY, Jr. and Betsey Harris. Married by Rev. Bernard Todd. Ministers' Returns p 40

31 August 1813. Isham HARVEY and Betsey Harris, dau. Robert Harris who is surety. (Same as above?). p 510

9 May 1782. Joel HARVEY (Hanoy?) and Nancy Claton. Married by Rev. John Weatherford. Ministers' Returns p 3

3 September 1792. Nathan HARVEY and Mary Williamson, dau. Cuthbert Williamson. Sur. Anthony Philips. Nathan son of Thomas Harvey. See Nathan Haney. p 182

3 June 1789. Thomas HARVEY and Nancy Buckner. Sur. Josiah Foster, Jr. p 135

18 May 1790. William P. HARVEY and Milly Brown. Sur. James Brown.
p 146

17 November 1815. Edward HASKINS and Anne G. Finch, dau. Zacharish
Finch. Sur. Drury Bacon. p 531

2 March 1795. Bartlett HATCHETT and Peggy Russell, dau. Edward Russell.
Sur. John Hatchett. Married 19 March by Rev. Archibald McRobert.
p 230

7 April 1813. Edward HATCHETT and Catherine Crutcher, dau. Reuben
Crutcher. Sur. James Crutcher. p 509

2 December 1793. John HATCHETT and Nancy Russell. Sur. William Dabbs.
Married 19 December by Rev. Drury Lacy. p 206

21 December 1803. John HATCHETT and Judith Foster, ward of William
Wilkes. Sur. Edward Hatchett. John son of Thomas Hatchett, Sr.
p 337

3 December 1787. William HATCHETT and Jane Roberts, dau. Francis Roberts.
Sur. John Roberts. Married 13 December by Rev. Thomas Johnston who
says Jeane. p 102

20 July 1793. William HATCHETT and Sally Turner. Sur. Martin Turner.
p 206

17 November 1797. David HATFIELD and Peggy Hawkins. Sur. Josiah
Foster. See David Harefield. p 251

28 August 1806. Jesse HATTON and Sarah Ward, dau. Joseph Ward who is
surety. Married same day by Rev. John Chappell. p 393

27 October 1788. Reuben HAY and Elizabeth Fuqua, dau. John Fuqua who is
surety. Married 30 October by Rev. Thomas Johnston. p 117

22 October 1789. Thomas HAY and Elizabeth Haley, dau. John Haley. Sur.
Reuben Haley. Married same day by Rev. John Easter. p 136

18 April 1782. James HAYES and Elizabeth Clayton. Married by Rev.
John Weatherford. Ministers' Returns p 3

7 June 1785. James HAYES and Martha Grigg. Sur. Matthew White. James
son of Richard Hayes. Married 30 June by Rev. Thomas Johnston. p 71

27 December 1790. Samuel HAZELRIGG and Martha Holt, dau. Rachel Holt.
Sur. Godfrey Jones, Jr. p 153

7 August 1780. Benjamin HAZELWOOD and Catherine Harroway. Sur. Charles
Harroway. p 38

4 June 1787. Benjamin HAZELWOOD and Sally Cox, dau. John and Sarah Cox.
Sur. William Hazelwood. See William Hazelwood. p 103

22 September 1782. Luke HAZELWOOD and Sarah Harroway. Married by Rev.
John Weatherford. Ministers' Returns p 2

8 February 1804. Luke HAZELWOOD, Jr. and Jincy Davenport, dau. Martin Davenport. Sur. George Davenport. Luke son of Luke Hazelwood, Sr. Married 11 February by Rev. John Chappell. p 352

6 February 1786. William HAZELWOOD and Sally Cox. Married by Rev. John Weatherford. See Benjamin Hazelwood. Ministers' Returns p 6

6 November 1788. Reuben HEARNDON and Fanny Kennady. Married by Rev. John Williams. Ministers' Returns p 9

20 November 1800. John HEATON and Martha Thompson. Married by Rev. Obadiah Edge. Ministers' Returns p 25

16 September 1805. Kelley HEATON and Elizabeth McCargo. Sur. John Heaton. Married 17 September by Rev. Obadiah Edge. p 376

26 July 1806. Silas HEATON and Sally Lewis, dau. Charles Lewis. Sur. Robert Lewis. p 393

2 November 1807. James HELM and Mary O. Chapman, dau. Benjamin Chapman who is surety. Married 5 November by Rev. John Chappell. p 407

18 January 1814. C. C. G. HENDERSON and Betsy Morton, dau. Jacob Morton. Sur. Richard W. Gaines. p 516

26 October 1783. Elijah HENDRICK and Anne Harrison, dau. Thomas Harrison. Sur. Nelson Calvert. Married 27 October by Rev. Thomas Johnston. p 82

10 February 1813. Thomas HENDRICKS and Sally Tankersley, dau. John Tankersley. Sur. Archibald Haley. Married 11 February by Rev. Richard Dabbs. p 508

17 July 1798. Edward HENRY and Martha Catherine Henry, dau. Patrick Henry. Sur. John D. Johnson. p 274

23 June 1809. Benjamin HERNDON and Cisley Neal. Sur. Hezekiah McCargo. Married 27 June by Rev. Richard Dabbs. p 443

30 December 1784. Edmund HERNDON and Letty Moseley, dau. Edward Moseley. Sur. Hillery Moseley. Married 4 January 1785, by Rev. Thomas Johnston. p 62

19 April 1788. John HERNDON and Jensey Kennady, dau. John Kennady. Sur. William Bryant. See John Hudson. p 115

2 December 1805. John HERNDON and Elizabeth Mealer. Sur. Francis Roberts. Married 12 December by Rev. Edward Almond. p 370

29 March 1794. Joseph HERNDON and Mary Rolings (widow). Sur. John Rollings. Married 3 April by Rev. John Williams. p 219

4 November 1788. Reuben HERNDON and Fanny Kennady. Sur. John Kennady. Married 6 November by Rev. John Williams. p 118

23 December 1790. Thomas HEWITT and Fanny Hines, dau. Calop Hines. Sur. John Hewitt. p 150

22 December 1790. Warner HEWITT and Betsey Sublett, dau. Benjamin
Sublett. Sur. Henry Hines. Warner son of John Hewitt. Married
23 December by Rev. Joshua Worley. p 140

27 December 1803. Warner HEWITT and Mary Hunter, dau. John Hunter.
Sur. Alexander Hunter. Married 29 December by Rev. Joshua Worley.
p 337

26 February 1787. Freeman HIGH and Elizabeth Beasley, dau. John
Beasley. Sur. David High. Married by Rev. Thomas Johnston who says
27 July. p 102

2 January 1787. Isom HIGH and Anna Martin, dau. Abraham Martin who is
surety. Married 3 January by Rev. Edward Almond. p 102

9 May 1798. Westmoreland HIGH and Polly Short Hames. Sur. William
Hames. Married 15 May by Rev. Edward Almond. p 269

2 February 1801. Edward HIGHT and Elizabeth Smith, dau. Isaac Smith.
Sur. William Adams. Edward son of Richard Hight. p 301

2 Spetember 1793. Richard HIGHT and Mary Ann Morton (widow). Sur.
George Smith. Returned October 1793 Court by Rev. John Chappell.
p 194

19 September 1782. Thomas HIGHT and Priscilla May, sister of Stephen
May. Sur. George Redd. p 46

6 May 1815. John HIGHTOWER and Polly Smith, dau. William Smith. Sur.
Flanders Tyree. p 524

26 February 1788. John HILL and Biddy Totty, dau. William Totty.
Sur. John Harris. p 116

5 October 1792. William HILL and Nancy Morton. Sur. Benjamin Morton.
Married 15 October by Rev. Drury Lacy. p 184

10 November 1783. Richard HILLIARD and Sarah Stark. Married by Rev.
Thomas Johnston. See Richard Hilyard. Ministers' Returns p 4

10 November 1783. Richard HILYARD and Sarah Stark, dau. Thomas Stark.
Sur. Edward Keeling. See Richard Hilliard. p 59

6 December 1784. James HINES and Polly Brown, dau. William Brown. Sur.
Thomas North. Married 23 October (?) by Rev. John Weatherford. p 66

19 March 1795. John HINES and Sally Davis. Married by Rev. Joshua
Worley. Ministers' Returns p 19

1 December 1788. William HINES and Nancy Harris, dau. Charles Harris.
Sur. John McMichael. p 116

3 April 1786. Russell HITCHCOCK and Anne Brown, dau. William Brown
who is surety. p 96

30 January 1804. Nathaniel B. HIX and Elizabeth A. Vernon, dau.
Richard Vernon who is surety. p 353

10 June 1802. Edmund HOARD and Polly Whitlow. Married by Rev. Edward
Almond. See Edmund Hard. Ministers' Returns p 28

8 January 1806. John HOARD and Martha Stokes Neal, dau. Thomas Neal.
Sur. William Hord. Married 14 January by Rev. William Richards. p 393

7 June 1779. Thomas HOARD and Mary Cargill. p 36

26 January 1784. Benjamin HODNETT and Betsey Collier, dau. Benjamin and
Sarah Collier. Sur. Fontaine Tankersley. Married 28 January by
Rev. Thomas Johnston. p 63

24 October 1803. Moses HOGE and Susanna Hunt, widow of William P. Hunt.
Sur. Henry A. Watkins. p 336

21 February 1779. James HOLLOWAY and Martha Owen Spencer, dau. Thomas
Spencer. Sur. Thomas Spencer, Jr. p 35

22 December 1807. Lewis HOLLOWAY and Sally Jones, dau. Codwallader
Jones who is surety. Married 24 December by Rev. Richard Dabbs, Jr.
p 407

21 May 1789. Daniel HOLT and Prudence Worsham, dau. Robert Williamson.
Married 23 May by Rev. John Williams. Sur. Jacob Williamson. p 134

2 October 1815. Jesse HOLT and Sarah Foster. Sur. Ludson Foster.
Married 5 October by Rev. James Robertson. p 535

1 February 1773. John White HOLT and Luisy (Louisa) Watson, dau.
Matthew Watson. Sur. Robert Williams. p 20

1 June 1778. Joseph HOLT and Sarah Garden. Sur. Sackville Brewer. p 31

6 February 1797. Thomas HOLT and Jane Bailey, dau. David Bailey. Sur.
William Bryant. Married by Rev. Archibald Alexander. p 250

10 November 1806. William HOLT and Elizabeth Bailey, dau. Mary Bailey.
Sur. Carloss Wood. William son of Robert Holt. Married 27 November
by Rev. Richard Dabbs, Jr. p 389

4 February 1815. William HOLT and Sophea W. Maloney, dau. James
Maloney who is surety. p 532

26 January 1809. William HOWARD and Nancy Clark. Sur. William Clark.
p 436

8 February 1803. James HOWELL and Nancy Bottom. Married by Rev. Edward
Almond. See James Powell. Ministers' Returns p 30

29 April 1812. John HOWELL and Susanna Austin. Sur. William S.
Carwiles. Married 30 April by Rev. Joshua Worley. p 488

25 December 1808. Mathew HOWELL and Mildred Byrd. Married by Rev.
Joseph Jenkins. Ministers' Returns p 37

7 May 1804. Benjamin HOWLETT and Sarah Allen, dau. John Allen, Sr.
Sur. Thomas Toombs. p 363

30 October 1797. Benjamin HUDSON and Lucy Bartee, dau. Phoebe Bartee.
Sur. John Davis. p 250

30 December 1784. Cuthbert HUDSON and Lucy Goodwyn. Married by Rev.
Thomas Johnston. Ministers' Returns p 4

22 May 1788. David HUDSON and Mary Cobbs Booker, dau. William Booker
who is surety. Married 23 November by Rev. Thomas Johnston.
p 116

26 April 1788. John HUDSON and Jincey Kennady. Married by Rev. Edward
Almond. See John Hearndon. Ministers' Returns p 10

2 August 1813. William R. HUDSON and Winnefred R. Webb, dau. Thomas
Webb who is surety. Married 7 August by Rev. William Richards.
p 508

1 November 1782. Henry HUGHES and Janey Haines. Married by Rev.
Thomas Johnston. Ministers' Returns p 1

5 March 1810. John HUGHES and Lucy Dennis. Sur. John Oliver. p 456

6 February 1809. John B. HUGHES and Nancy Hughes, dau. John Hughes.
Sur. Jesse Hughes. John B. Hughes of Amherst County. p 457

10 January 1811. John M. HUGHES and Betsey Michael, dau. Archer
Michael. Sur. John Michael. Married 11 January by Rev. John
Chappell. p 471

2 January 1783. William HUGHES and Lucy Greenwood. Married by Rev.
Thomas Johnston. Ministers' Returns p 2

30 June 1771. Samuel HUMPHRIES and Rachel Humphries, dau. Daniel
Humphries. Sur. David Humprhies. p 11

2 March 1795. John HUNDLEY and Elizabeth Edge, dau. Obadiah Edge.
Sur. William Smith. Married 12 March by Rev. Joshua Worley. p 223

30 January 1812. James HUNT, Jr. and Edith Mullings, dau. William
Mullings. James, Jr. son of James Hunt, Sr. Married same day by
Rev. Williams Fears. p 488

19 December 1787. Gilbert HUNT and Sarah Hoard. Sur. Williamson Price.
Married 20 December by Rev. Thomas Johnston. p 98

13 April 1790. William Pitt HUNT and Susanna Watkins, dau. Joel Watkins.
Sur. Edmund Read. Married 16 April by Rev. John B. Smith. p 145

1 May 1786. Alexander HUNTER and Nancy Marshall, dau. Benjamin and
Hannah Marshall. Sur. Andrew Wallace. p 91

5 December 1796. Adam HUNTSMAN and Nancy Pugh (widow). Sur. Thomas
Read. Married 29 December by Rev. William Dameron. p 236

20 March 1782. Jacob HUNTSMAN and Mary Devine. Sur. James Speed.
Married 23 March by Rev. Thomas Johnston. p 48

20 June 1787. Jacob HUNTSMAN and Elizabeth Hunt, dau. Charles and Tabitha Hunt. Sur. William Henry Patillo. Married 25 June by Rev. John Weatherford. p 98

18 June 1805. James HUNTSMAN and Mary Farmer, dau. Stephen Farmer who is surety. Married 20 June by Rev. John Chappell. p 377

21 December 1815. Samuel HUNTSMAN and Sarah R. Cheatham, dau. William Cheatham. Sur. Charles W. Cheatham. Married same day by Rev. John Chappell. p 531

15 January 1792. Collier HUTCHESON and Sarah Gaines Collier, dau. John Collier. Sur. Harrison Munday. Married 19 January by Rev. John Williams. p 176

17 September 1804. Collier HUTCHESON and Sally Williams, dau. Thomas and Frances Williams. Sur. Robert Williams. Married 18 September by Rev. Thomas Hardie. p 353

7 November 1808. David HUTCHESON and Hannah Marshall, dau. Benjamin Marshall who is surety. p 427

17 October 1796. Matthew HUTCHESON and Ruth Brizendine, dau. William Brizendine. Sur. James Ashworth. Married 25 October by Rev. Edward Almond. p 236

27 July 1801. Matthew HUTCHESON and Nancy Whitlow (widow). Sur. William Brizendine. p 301

4 November 1811. Samuel HUTCHESON and Sally Marshall, dau. Benjamin Marshall who is surety. Married 14 November by Rev. Joshua Worley. p 472

26 May 1801. James INGE and Amy Diggs, dau. John Diggs who is surety. Married 28 May by Rev. Edward Almond who says Amy **Biggs**. p 304

2 July 1796. Joseph B. INGRAM and Elizabeth Collier, dau. Thomas Collier. Sur. Collier Hutcheson. Married 21 July by Rev. Edward Almond. p 236

2 September 1805. Joseph B. INGRAM and Patsey May, ward of Allen Gilliam who is surety. Married 18 September by Rev. Edward Almond. p 376

1 April 1805. David IRBY and Lucy Hudson, dau. Daniel and Tabitha Hudson. Sur. Jacob Hudson. Married 3 April by Rev. William Richards. p 374

4 January 1813. Gerald IBRY and Martha Woodfin, dau. George Woodfin who is surety. Married 14 January by Rev. Richard Dabbs. p 510

6 June 1785. Cain JACKSON and Elizabeth Claybrook, dau. Obadiah Claybrook who is surety. Married 9 June by Rev. Thomas Johnston. p 71

13 October 1777. Cain JACKSON and Drucilla Allen. Sur. Lewis Jackson. p 28

3 December 1792. Francis JACKSON and Elizabeth Rice. Sur. John Clarkson. p 184

4 September 1797. John JACKSON and Mary Staples (widow). Sur. Hillery Moseley. p 258

3 December 1802. John JACKSON and Salley Holloway, dau. John Holloway. Sur. John L. Jackson. Married 14 December by Rev. William Spencer. p 317

5 August 1785. Josiah JACKSON and Susanna Fuqua, dau. John Fuqua. Sur. Robert Jackson. Married 9 August by Rev. Thomas Johnston. p 80

30 March 1790. Josiah JACKSON and Elizabeth Madison, dau. Henry Madison. Sur. Thomas Pettus. Married 1 April by Rev. John Weatherford. p 151

13 May 1811. Lewis JACKSON and Elizabeth Hines, widow of Henry Hines. Sur. James Philips. Married 14 May by Rev. Bernard Todd. p 470

7 March 1804. Ralph JACKSON and Polly Harvey, dau. Thomas Harvey. Sur. Isham Harvey. Married same day by Obadiah Edge. p 355

22 November 1815. Thomas JACKSON, Jr. and Nancy Clark, dau. Elijah Clark. Sur. Harrison Vernon. Thomas, Jr. son of Thomas Jackson, Sr. p 526

2 January 1792. George JAMES and Charlotte Connelly, dau. James Connelly. Sur. John James. Married 28 December 1791 (?) by Rev. Edward Almond. p 170

1 April 1791. John JAMES and Priscilla Ward, dau. Catherine Ward. Sur. Cyrus Connely. Married 12 April by Rev. Edward Almond. p 164

24 December 1793. Clement R. JAMESON and Elizabeth Elliott, dau. Richard Elliott. Sur. John Morris. Edmund Read guardian of Clement R. Jameson. Married 26 December by Rev. John Weatherford. p 203

23 December 1806. Edmund JAMESON and Nancy Scott, dau. Francis Scott. Sur. William Copeland. p 392

9 December 1768. William JAMESON and Anne Read, dau. Clement Read. Sur. Thomas Read. p 6

7 December 1812. Jennings M. JEFFREYS and Peggy Moseley, dau. Hillery Moseley. Sur. Henry F. Farley. Married 9 December by Rev. William Richards. p 491

20 October 1803. Richard JEFFREYS and Nancy Hamlett, dau. James Hamlett. Sur. James Wilson (Double Wedding!) Married same day by Rev. Edward Almond. p 331

9 August 1794. Thomas JEFFREYS and Polly Hamlett, dau. James Hamlett. Sur. Thomas Walker. Married 2 September by Rev. John Williams. p 219

27 March 1804. Achilles JEFFRIES and Susanna P. Williamson, dau. Cuthbert Williamson. Sur. John Williamson. p 355

28 February 1815. Richard L. JEFFRIES and Priscilla F. May. Sur. Allen Gilliam. p 527

18 January 1791. Cain JENNINGS and Esther Baldwin, dau. Caleb Baldwin. Sur. Temple Davis. Married 20 January by Rev. Joshua Worley. p 157

8 January 1796. George JENNINGS and Frances Jackson. Sur. Peter Stern.
George son of Dickerson Jennings. p 263

18 June 1805. James JENNINGS and Rachel Holloway, dau. John Holloway.
Sur. Francis Jackson. Married 23 June by Rev. Joshua Worley. p 378

7 December 1812. Jesse JENNINGS and Rebecca Richardson, dau. John
Richardson. Sur. Ralph Merriman. p 483

5 December 1804. Paschall JENNINGS and Sarah Thornton, dau. Francis
Thornton who is surety. Married 15 December by Rev. Joshua Worley.
p 356

3 January 1791. Pleasants JENNINGS and Betsey Harvey, dau. Thomas
Harvey who is surety. p 157

11 December 1806. Thomas E. JETER and Sally B. Chappell, dau. John
Chappell. Sur. Hugh Reese. Married same day by Rev. John Chappell.
p 387

4 November 1799. Anthony JOHNS and Sarah Oliver, dau. Thomas Oliver
who is surety. Married 7 November by Rev. John Chappell. p 278

3 November 1794. Thomas JOHNS and Frankey Claybrook. Sur. Obadiah
Claybrook. p 219

4 June 1792. Daniel JOHNSON and Nancy Roach. Sur. Abraham King.
Married 7 June by Rev. Henry Lester. p 185

21 July 1802. Jesse JOHNSON and Letty Green, dau. John Green. Sur.
Grissett Green. Wit. Croxson Green. Married same day by Rev. John
Chappell. p 316

5 November 1798. John JOHNSON and Lucy Atkins, dau. Anne Atkins.
Sur. Thomas Atkins. p 270

21 July 1789. Josiah JOHNSON and Susanna Martin. Sur. Abraham Martin.
Married 24 July by Rev. Thomas Johnston. p 137

23 December 1797. Matthew JOHNSON and Jinsey Mullins, dau. James
Mullins who is surety. Married 26 December by Rev. Edward Almond.
p 258

21 December 1803. Michael JOHNSON and Peggy Williams, ward of W. M.
Watkins. Sur. Robert Williams. Michael son of Joshua Johnson.
Married 22 December by Rev. Edward Almond. p 347

24 December 1810. Nathan JOHNSON and Polly Minton, dau. Simeon H.
Minton who is surety. Married 27 December by Rev. John Chappell.
p 456

30 June 1792. Reuben JOHNSON, Jr. and Susanna Foster. Sur. Reuben
Johnson, Sr. p 185

11 December 1800. Robert JOHNSON and Lucy Martin. Married by Rev.
Joshua Worley. Ministers' Returns p 27

23 July 1804. Robert JOHNSON and Peggy Lawson, dau. George Lawson.
Robert son of James Johnson who is surety. p 355

8 October 1798. Sias JOHNSON and Phelletia Hankins, widow of John Hankins. Sur. James Mullins. Married 11 October by Rev. Edward Almond. p 272

15 October 1803. William JOHNSON and Nancy Brewer (widow). Sur. John Moon. William son of Naom Johnson. Married same day by Rev. Obadiah Edge. p 348

23 July 1804. William JOHNSON and Martha Robertson. William son of James Johnson who is surety. p 356

11 August 1815. William JOHNSON and Nancy Burns. Married by Rev. William Richards. Ministers' Returns p 42

26 December 1809. James JOHNSTON, Jr. and Patsey R. Davenport, dau. Samuel Davenport. Sur. John Johnston. James, Jr. son of James Johnston, Sr. Married 28 December by Rev. Richard Dabbs. p 432

7 December 1811. Joshua JOHNSTON and Jane Pearson (widow). Sur. Thomas Hendrick. Married same day by Rev. Richard Dabbs. p 470

27 January 1797. Robert JOHNSTON and Betsey Mullins, dau. James Mullins who is surety. Married 2 February by Rev. Edward Almond. p 258

27 August 1806. Robert JOHNSTON and Mary Beadles, dau. William Beadles. Sur. Matthew Davenport. Married 28 August by Rev. Richard Dabbs, Jr. p 384

16 January 1792. Thomas JOHNSTON and Betsey Paulett. Sur. Thomas Paulett. Married 27 January by Rev. William Mahon. p 187

22 December 1780. William JOHNSTON and Rebecca Moseley. Sur. William Bouldin. p 41

2 April 1789. William JOHNSTON and Elizabeth Ford. Married by Rev. John Weatherford. Ministers' Returns p 11

9 November 1797. Cadwallader JONES and Mildred Jones. Married 9 January by Rev. William Dameron. Sur. Richard Jones. p 251

21 December 1812. Cadwallader JONES, Jr. and Polly Johnson, dau. John H. Johnson. Cadwallader, Jr. son of Cadwallader Jones, Sr. who is surety. p 488

15 January 1815. Cadwallader JONES, Jr. and Sallie Tatum, dau. Reuben Tatum. Sur. Cadwallader Jones, Sr. p 532

16 January 1809. Charles W. JONES and Elizabeth L. Daniel, dau. Campbell Daniel who is surety. Married 18 January by Rev. Richard Dabbs. p 437

23 September 1793. David JONES, Jr. and Rebecca Ford, dau. Culverine Ford. Sur. William Johnston. David son of David Jones, Sr. Married 2 December by Rev. John Weatherford. p 203

14 December 1795. David JONES and Elizabeth Johnson. Sur. John H. Johnson. Davis son of Godfrey Jones. Married 17 December by Rev. Archibald Alexander. p 230

17 December 1798. Dudley JONES and Annis Blankenship. Sur. John Blankenship. Married 19 December by Rev. Edward Almond. p 270

22 December 1802. Dudley JONES and Rachel Jones, dau. Richard Jones who is surety. p 316

24 August 1781. Godfrey JONES, Jr. and Elizabeth Holt, dau. William Holt. Sur. Dudley Holt. p 43

25 January 1813. James JONES and Polly Goode, dau. Mackness Goode. Sur. Richard R. Jones. p 511

21 February 1789. Lewellen JONES and Catherine Verner, dau. Ann Varner. Sur. Henry Pamplin. Lewellen son of Godfrey Jones. Married 26 February by Rev. William Mahon. p 129

17 September 1793. Nathaniel JONES and Mary Anne Varner, dau. Ann Varner. Nathaniel son of Godfrey Jones. Married by Rev. Henry Lester. p 202

14 September 1802. Peter JONES and Elizabeth Chastain. Sur. Isham Chastain. Wit. Isham and John Chastain. Married 16 September by Rev. Edward Almond. p 329

9 December 1811. Philip JONES, Esq. and Mary Petway Greenhill, ward of Francis Jones. Sur. David Greenhill. Married 19 December by Rev. John Chappell. p 469

26 June 1771. Richard JONES, Jr. and Lucy Clay, ward of Marston Clay. Richard son of Richard Jones, Sr. Sur. Richard Whitton, Jr. p 10

15 July 1785. Richard JONES and Amey Holt, dau. William Holt. Sur. Cadwallader Jones. Married by Rev. Thomas Johnston. p 72

14 October 1808. Richard JONES and Sally Jackson. Sur. Cadwallader Jones. Married 20 October by Rev. Joseph Jenkins. p 425

8 February 1811. Richard R. JONES and Betsey Goode, dau. Mackness Goode. Sur. William G. Goode. p 471.

12 April 1784. Robert JONES and Catherine Mullins. Married by the Rev. Thomas Johnston. Ministers' Returns p 2

18 December 1810. Robert JONES and Holly Johnson, dau. John H. Johnson. Sur. Cadwallader Jones. Married 20 December by Rev. Richard Dabbs who says Molly Johnston. p 456

13 October 1804. Short JONES and Mary W. Price, dau. William Price. Sur. Robert Price. Married 16 October by Rev. Richard Dabbs, Jr. p 354

1 November 1773. Thomas JONES and Katey Tankersley. Sur. John Tankersley. p 21

30 July 1793. Thomas JONES and Polly Clarkson. Sur. Thomas Holt. Married 1 August by Rev. Henry Lester. p 203

13 January 1808. Thomas JONES and Margaret Jones, dau. Godfrey Jones who is surety. Married 14 January by Rev. Richard Dabbs, Jr. p 421

18 April 1789. William JONES and Elizabeth Ford, dau. Culverine Ford who is surety. p 129

26 December 1804. William JONES and Lucy Tatum, dau. Reuben Tatum. Sur. Cadwallender Jones. Married 27 December by Rev. Richard Dabbs, Jr. p 354

4 February 1805. Elijah JORDAN and Martha Elizabeth Garland, ward of Peter Garland who is surety. Married 7 February by Rev. Obadiah Edge. p 379

3 August 1799. John JORDAN and Elizabeth Jordan, dau. Benjamin Jordan. Sur. Thomas Townsend. Married 8 August by Rev. John Chappell. p 279

23 December 1801. Reeves JORDAN and Jemima Bants. Sur. Matthew Sublett. Married by Rev. Joshua Worley who says Jamie Bollen. p 304

26 January 1793. Samuel JORDAN and Betsey Mills Jude. Sur. George Jude. Returned to May 1793 Court by Rev. John Chappell. p 204

7 November 1796. Samuel JORDAN and Ann Hudson Lewis, dau. Charles Lewis who is surety. p 243

14 January 1772. George JUDE and Anne Watson, dau. Matthew Watson who is surety. p 13

7 May 1813. William JUMPER and Polly Bird. Sur. Edmund Bird. p 509

6 January 1783. Joseph KATCHEN and Pattey Townsend, dau. John Townsend. Sur. John Wilson. See Joseph Kitchen. p 56

27 August 1767. Henry KAY and Anne Taylor, dau. James Taylor who is surety. p 4

26 August 1801. Richard KEIRSEY and Letty Worthy, dau. Martin Worthy. Sur. Thomas Tharp. Married 11 September by Rev. John Chappell. p 305

5 January 1797. William KEMP and Catey Roach, dau. John Roach. Sur. John Roach, Jr. p 252

8 September 1778. William KENNEDY and Mary Lindsay (widow). Sur. William Jameson. p 30

11 October 1814. Charles KENNON and Almeria Read, dau. Clement Read. Sur. Stephen Bedford. p 515

31 May 1791. Abraham KING and Mollie S. Roach, dau. John Roach who is surety. p 164

27 February 1792. Joseph KING and Patty Traynam, dau. William Traynam who is surety. Joseph son of Martin King. Married 3 March by Rev. Thomas Dobson. p 175

5 December 1798. John KINGSTON, Jr. and Sally Cayce, sister of
Micajah Cayce who is surety. John son of John Kingston, Sr. Married
13 December by Rev. John Chappell. p 272

7 September 1779. Drury KIRSEY and Patience Nunnaly, dau. Alexander and
Patience Nunnaly. Sur. Henry Eans. p 35

5 January 1783. Joseph KITCHEN and Patty Townsend. Married by Rev.
John Weatherford. See Joseph Katchen. Ministers' Returns p 3

8 February 1803. Edward LAINE and Betsy Williamson, dau. Jacob Williamson. Sur. Daniel Holt. Married 10 February by Rev. Edward Almond
who says Lane. p 332

6 January 1801. Jacob LAINE and Sarah Turner, ward of Stephen Turner
(brother). Sur. John Turner. p 300

24 January 1787. Leroy LAMBERT and Lydia Givins. Sur. James Stowe.
Married same day by Rev. John Williams. p 111

22 December 1786. Sterling LAMBERT and Mary High, dau. Daniel High who
is surety. Married 24 December by Rev. Thomas Johnston. p 89

16 December 1795. Sterling LAMBERT and Elizabeth Martin, dau. Jacob
Martin of Halifax County. Sur. James Downey. p 228

24 November 1783. James LAMKIN and Mary Dabbs, dau. Richard Dabbs who
is surety. See James Lampkin. p 58

26 November 1783. James LAMPKIN and Mary Dabbs. Married by the Rev.
Thomas Johnston. See James Lamkin. Minister' Returns p 1

13 August 1811. George T. LANSDAWN and Nancy Rudd. Sur. Charles H.
Slaughter. p 469

1 February 1790. Samuel LAUNDERMAN and Sally May. Sur. John May.
Married 11 February by Rev. John Williams. p 143

10 February 1768. John LAUNDERMAN and Martha Watson, dau. Edward Watson.
Sur. Thomas Read. Wit. on bond Jonathan Read. p 6

23 December 1805. Cheadle LAW and Nancy Hall, dau. Boller Hall. Sur.
John Brizendine. Married 24 December by Rev. William Richards. p 379

7 March 1796. Littleberry LAWRENCE and Hannah Jumper, dau. C. Jumper.
Sur. John Williamson. p 243

10 January 1786. Benjamin LAWSON and Phamey Traynum. Married by Rev.
Thomas Johnston. Ministers' Returns p 6

3 October 1785. George LAWSON and Sally Adams, dau. James Adams. Sur.
Claiborne Barksdale. Married 25 October by Rev. John Weatherford.
p 72

1 November 1813. James LAWSON and Sally Pugh, dau. John Pugh who is
surety. Married 11 November by Rev. John Chappell. p 511

6 November 1793. Joshua LAWSON and Elizabeth Dickerson. Sur. Benjamin Lawson. Married 14 November by Rev. John Williams. p 188

20 August 1802. Nathan LAWSON and Christian High. Sur. Westmoreland High. Married 26 August by Rev. John Ligon. p 319

10 March 1785. Zachariah LAWSON and Agnes Jones. Married by Rev. Thomas Johnston. Ministers' Returns p 5

8 December 1802. Zachariah LAWSON and Ava Wilson (widow). Sur. Elisha Williams. Married 21 December by Rev. Thomas Dobson. p 319

15 September 1795. William LEA and Nancy Hundley, dau. George Hundley. Sur. William Trevatt. p 228

2 December 1806. William LEAGUE and Sally Turner. Sur. Benjamin Oliver. p 388

7 December 1804. John LEASON and Susannah Hanaway. Married by Rev. John Chappell. See John Leeson. Ministers' Returns p 32

10 October 1792. William LEATHMAN and Elizabeth Holloway. Married by Rev. John Williams. See William Loathman. Ministers' Returns p 15

11 February 1812. John LEE and Frances Webb (widow). Sur. Charles H. Pearson. Married 12 February by Rev. Richard Dabbs. p 487

7 December 1804. John LEESON and Susanna Harroway. Sur. Ezekiah Mann. See John Leason. p 359

22 October 1808. Nash LE GRANDE and Pauline Read (widow). Sur. Thomas Read. p 418

24 January 1792. George LEONARD and Olivia Brown, dau. William Brown. Sur. William Raymond. p 181

16 May 1782. - LEPONT and Nancy Pady. Sur. Culverine Ford. Request of - Lepant in French. Married 18 May by Rev. Thomas Johnston who says Mary Rady. p 51

2 October 1806. John LESSEUR and Nancy Timberlake, dau. John Timberlake. Sur. John Dennis. Married by Rev. Clement Read. p 388

30 March 1808. Bryant W. LESTER and Elizabeth Friend, dau. Joseph Friend, Sr. Sur. Joseph Friend, Jr. p 415

3 November 1771. Henry LESTER and Betsey McConnies. Henry son of Bryant Lester. Sur. Christopher McConnies. p 10

3 May 1812. Corbin LEWIS and Nancy Dabbs, dau. William Dabbs. Sur. Charles R. Slaughter. p 491

17 April 1809. Edgecombe L. LEWIS and Anne Davenport, dau. Richard Davenport. Sur. Ballard Davenport. Married 22 April by Rev. John Chappell. p 432

23 November 1812. Peter LEWIS and Mary Smith Buster (widow?), dau. John Smith. Sur. William S. Chappell. Married 26 November by Rev. John Chappell. p 487

7 January 1805. Robert LEWIS and Martha Greenhill, ward of Samuel Jordan who is surety. Robert son of Charles Lewis. Married 9 January by Rev. John Chappell. p 379

6 October 1806. Warner LEWIS and Milly V. Hundley. Sur. Richard Lipscomb. Married same day by Rev. Richard Dabbs, Jr. p 388

12 November 1812. John LIGON and Nancy Daniel, dau. Campbell Daniel. Sur. Robert Blanks. p 487

13 December 1780. Thomas LIGON and Fanny Bumpass. Sur. James Hamlett. p 38

5 August 1782. Francis LINDSAY and Sarah Roberts. Sur. Thomas Collier. Married same day by Rev. Thomas Johnston. p 47

24 December 1794. Wright LINDSEY and Sarah Roberts. Sur. James Shelton. Wright son of Francis Lindsey. p 215

4 December 1800. George LIPSCOMB and Polly Morton. Married by Rev. John Chappell. Ministers' Returns p 25

1 March 1811. Jason LIPSCOMB and Nancy Hood, dau. Sterling Hood. Sur. Cornelius Beasley. p 469

8 April 1801. Temple LIPSCOMB and Milly Lipscomb, dau. Richard G. Lipscomb who is surety. Married 9 April by Rev. Thomas Dobson. p 306

27 September 1772. John LIPSCOMBE and Margaret Almond, dau. John Almond. Sur. John May. p 20

20 March 1773. Thomas LIPSCOMBE and Mary Barksdale, dau. Collier Barksdale who is surety. p 20

30 November 1792. William LOATHMAN and Elizabeth Holloway, dau. George Holloway. Sur. Brooks Robertson. See William Leathman. p 175

19 November 1799. Thomas LOCKETT and Susanna Blanks, dau. John Blanks. Sur. Francis Lockett. Married 26 November by Rev. William Richards. p 281

18 December 1810. Saunders LOGGINS and Elizabeth Hailey, dau. Joseph Hailey. p 449

18 July 1792. Adam LOVING and Patty Arnold, dau. James Arnold. Sur. Archibald Campbell. Married 19 July by Rev. Edward Almond. p 175

21 February 1809. Adam LOVING and Polly Gibbons, dau. Elizabeth Gibbons. Sur. William Eudaly. p 438

4 May 1810. Benjamin LOVING and Jinsey Kenady, dau. John Kenady who is surety. Married 10 May by Rev. Richard Dabbs who says Jane Canady. p 459

20 March 1787. James LOVING and Frances Clements, dau. Benjamin Clements who is surety. Married 22 March by Rev. John Williams. p 100

16 December 1788. Richard LOVING and Frances Blankenship, dau. John Blankenship. Sur. Levy Blankenship. Married 18 December by Rev. Thomas Johnston. p 124

21 October 1799. George LOWELL and Polly Hannah, dau. Rebecca Hannah. Sur. William Spencer. p 276

5 March 1810. Gideon LUCAS and Patsey Mitchell, dau. Thomas Mitchell who is surety. p 449

8 December 1786. Moses LUCAS and Sally Comer, dau. Samuel Comer. Sur. Hugh Comer. Moses son of William Lucas. Both parties from Orange County. Married 9 December by Rev. Thomas Johnston. p 89

21 June 1797. John LUMPKIN and Lucresy Martin, dau. Samuel Martin who is surety. John son of Anney Lumpkin. Married 26 June by Rev. Obadiah Edge who says Luraney. p 252

17 December 1798. William LUNDERMAN and Winifred Vaughan, dau. Zedekiah Vaughan. Sur. Robert Johnson. Married 20 December by Rev. Joshua Worley. p 271

23 November 1793. Samuel LYLE and Nancy Harrison, dau. Moses Harrison. Sur. John Norris. Married 24 November by Rev. John Williams. p 202

31 August 1790. Dr. George LYNN and Anne Woodson Venable, dau. James Venable. Sur. Joseph Venable. Married 2 September by Rev. William Mahon. p 138

4 January 1790. Thomas MACKEY and Anne Fuqua, dau. Samuel Fuqua. Sur. Jacob Morton. Married 10 July (?) by Rev. John Weatherford. p 141

6 August 1810. Michael MADDOX and Raney Crawley. Sur. William Crawley. Married same day by Rev. Richard Dabbs. p 450

9 July 1810. Henry MADISON and Elizabeth White, ward of Nathan Harvey who is surety. p 450

12 March 1785. William MAHON and Agnes Venable, dau. James Venable who is surety. p 73

19 May 1784. Perry MAHONEY and Sarah Vaughan, dau. Abraham Vaughan who consents. Sur. John Bram. Married same day by Rev. Thomas Johnston. p 65

16 October 1809. William MAJOR and Obedience Hamlett, dau. James Hamlett, Sr. Sur. James Hamlett, Jr. Married 25 October by Rev. Richard Dabbs. p 444

3 February 1802. John MALONE and Patsey King (widow). Sur. Reuben Traynum. Married same day by Rev. Thomas Dobson. p 321

11 March 1795. Hezekiah MANN and Susanna Martin, sister of George Coleman Martin who is surety. Married 12 March by Rev. Edward Almond. p 222

8 November 1788. Jesse MANN and Nancy Perkinson, dau. Seth Perkinson who is surety. Jesse son of Samuel Mann. Married 13 November by Rev. John Williams. p 123

13 November 1795. Robert MANN and Mary Bevill. Sur. Seth Perkinson. Married 14 November by Rev. Edward Almond. p 225

16 December 1805. William MANN and Anne Goode, dau. Philip Goode. Sur. Delanson Goode. Married same day by Rev. Thomas Hardie. p 380

18 August 1775. Nathaniel MANSON and Lucy W. Clayton, dau. John Clayton who is surety. p 27

1 December 1788. William MANSON, Jr. and Elizabeth Scates, dau. William Scates. Sur. William Manson. p 124

8 January 1799. Richard MARABLE and Sarah Billups, sister of Capt. John Billups. Sur. John Marable. Married 10 January by Rev. William Richards who says Sarah Givin Billups. p 282

30 August 1806. Benjamin MARRABLE and Sarah Bibb, dau. John Bibb. Sur. Josiah Moseley. Benjamin son of George Marrable. Married same day by Rev. William Richards. p 387

24 September 1782. Benjamin MARSHALL and Sarah Pulliam, daughter-in-law (step-dau.) of William Davenport. Sur. Richard Davenport. Married 27 September by Rev. John Weatherford. p 49

3 July 1815. James P. MARSHALL and Elizabeth E. Watkins, dau. Henry A. Watkins. Sur. John H. Marshall. p 530

13 April 1813. John H. MARSHALL and Jincey Morton, dau. William Morton. Sur. Hillery Moseley, Jr. p 495

5 April 1813. John W. MARSHALL and Mary Hancock, dau. Martin Hancock. Sur. Benjamin Marshall. p 504

1 January 1790. William MARSHALL and Mary Ann Gaines, dau. Richard Gaines. Sur. William Gaines. Married 14 July (?) by Rev. William Mahon. p 138

17 June 1813. William MARSHALL and Polly Goode Gilliam, dau. Allen Gilliam. Sur. Henry Barnes. p 495

21 February 1780. Barkley MARTIN and Rebecca Clay, dau. Henry Clay. Sur. William Vaughan. p 38

7 April 1794. Hudson MARTIN and Elizabeth Moore. Sur. George Martin. p 215

15 February 1786. James MARTIN and Mary Martin. Married by Rev. John Weatherford. Ministers' Returns p 6

25 June 1791. George Coleman MARTIN and Lucy Atkins, dau. John Atkins, Sr. Sur. Willliam Hawkins. Married 26 June by Rev. John Williams. p 164

26 December 1774. John MARTIN and Anne Spencer, dau. Thomas Spencer. Sur. Sion Spencer. p 24

7 March 1787. Matthew MARTIN and Sally Clay, dau. Henry and Polly Clay who consent. Sur. Thomas Flournoy. Married 8 March by Rev. John Williams. p 97

14 February 1810. Claiborn MASON and Betsey McDearmon, dau. Thomas McDearmon. Sur. Joseph Mason. p 457

11 March 1812. Jesse MASON and Patsey Weatherford, dau. John Weatherford. Sur. Charles A. Weatherford. p 481

29 August 1792. John MASON and Keziah Fore, dau. John Fore. Sur. George Fore. Married 30 August by Rev. Joshua Worley. p 177

22 September 1807. John MASON and Winifred Graves, dau. William Graves. Sur. Leonard Barnes. p 405

30 December 1803. Joseph MASON and Elizabeth Weatherford, dau. John Weatherford. Sur. John W. Weatherford. p 346

20 December 1809. Obadiah MASON and Louisa Weatherford, dau. John Weatherford. Sur. Josiah Mason. p 439

20 November 1792. Peter MASON and Elizabeth Fore. Sur. George Fore. Peter son of William Mason. Married 29 November by Rev. Joshua Worley. p 176

17 November 1807. William MASON and Nancy McDearman, dau. Dudley McDearman. Sur. Asa Holt. William Mason of Campbell County. p 405

11 February 1791. John MATTHEWS and Sarah White. Sur. James Haney. p 165

12 March 1791. John MATTHEWS and Sarah White (widow). Sur. William Dabbs. (Both marriages given). p 162

13 March 1791. John MATTHEWS and Sarah Childress. Married by Rev. John Williams. (Probably Sarah (Childress) White, widow). Ministers' Returns p 14

6 December 1803. John MATTHEWS and Elizabeth Daniel, dau. John Daniel. Sur. Stephen Bedford. p 347

17 October 1805. John MATTHEWS and Mary Brizendine, dau. William Brizendine. Sur. Joel Ashworth. Married 19 October by Rev. William Richards. p 380

15 March 1791. Samuel MATTHEWS and Anne Rudd, (widow). Sur. Bernard Cheatham. p 167

26 August 1812. Thomas MATTHEWS and Kitty Hughs, dau. John Hughs. Sur. Richard Clark. p 479

4 October 1784. David MAY and Mary Mullins, Jr., dau. Mary Mullins. Sur. James Mullins. Married 14 October by Rev. Thomas Johnston. p 62

5 November 1787. Edmund MAY and Dorcas Lunderman, sister of Samuel Lunderman who is surety. Married 14 November by Rev. John Williams. p 97

6 October 1783. Stephen MAY and Elizabeth Gilliam, dau. James Gilliam. Sur. Abner May. Married 10 October by Rev. Thomas Johnston. p 57

5 October 1801. Woodson MAY and Elizabeth Lee (widow). Sur. Carter White. Married 10 October by Rev. Edward Almond. p 307

9 December 1814. John G. MAYNE and Susanna Cheaney, dau. Susanna Cheaney. Sur. James Cheaney. p 517

11 December 1811. Nathanial MEADOWS and Sarah Duffer, dau. Isaac and Martha Duffer. Sur. Samuel Davis. p 465

2 December 1793. George MEANLEY and Judy Mimms, dau. Mary Mims. Sur. John Mims. Married 5 December by Rev. Edward Almond. p 194

6 January 1783. George MERCE (Meree?) and Mary Bailey. Married by Rev. Thomas Johnston. Ministers' Returns p 1

19 December 1810. Ralph MERRIMAN and Patsey Richardson, dau. John Richardson. Sur. Thomas Merriman. p 457

13 April 1813. John MICHAEL and Jinsey Hames, dau. William Hames who is surety. Married 16 April by Rev. Thomas E. Jeter. p 504

17 November 1781. James MIDDLETON and Sarah Love, dau. John Love. Sur. William Morton. p 43

14 September 1791. David MILLER and Elizabeth Tarpley, dau. James Tarpley. Sur. Lewis Hammock. Married 15 September by Rev. Edward Almond. p 160

11 January 1793. James MILLER and Frances Carter. Sur. Matthew White. Married 23 January by Rev. William Mahon. p 194

3 August 1807. John MILLER and Polly Gaines, dau. Thomas Gaines. Sur. Richard W. Gaines. p 405

6 August 1781. Smith MILLER and Martha Rawlins, dau. Peter Rawlins. Sur. Lewellen Jones. p 42

9 July 1804. Henry MILLS and Judith Brizendine, widow of Abner Brizendine. Sur. John Paul Redd. Married 13 July by Rev. Richard Dabbs, Jr. p 356

28 September 1775. Mathew MILLS and Sarah Challice, dau. H. Challice. Sur. William Watson. Wit. to consent Martha Challis and Fanny Wagner Challis. p 26

3 December 1787. Moses MILLS and Keron Happock Rather, dau. James and Lucy Rather. Sur. Francis Clark. Married 8 December by Rev. Joshua Worley. p 97

18 November 1795. George MILUM and Jinsey Crafton, dau. Anthony and Mary Crafton. Sur. Richard Rutledge. Married 20 November by Rev. Edward Almond. p 222

24 December 1810. Simon H. MINTON and Frances Roberts (widow). Sur. Wylie Roberts. Married 27 December by Rev. John Chappell. p 457

7 January 1788. James MITCHELL and Sarah Phelps, dau. John Phelps who is surety. p 123

3 October 1803. James MITCHELL and Frances Ferguson. Sur. William Floyd. Married 2 November by Rev. Joshua Worley. p 346

28 October 1786. Richard MITCHELL and Elizabeth Morgan, dau. Robert Morgan who is surety. p 90

10 January 1789. Thomas MITCHELL and Nancy Almond, dau. Emanuel Almond. Sur. George Fore. Married 15 January by Rev. Joshua Worley. p 132

7 November 1797. Thomas MITCHELL and Polly Mitchell, dau. Randall Mitchell. Sur. Richard Dabbs, Jr. p 252

3 October 1807. Walter MITCHELL and Elizabeth Dabbs, dau. James Dabbs. Sur. Josiah Foster. Married 8 October by Rev. Richard Dabbs, Jr. p 408

1 February 1790. William MITCHELL and Elizabeth Singleton Dabbs, dau. Richard Dabbs. Sur. George Dabbs. Married 18 February by Rev. Henry Lester. p 144

2 October 1786. William MONDAY and Nancy Staples, dau. William Staples. Sur. Joel Ashworth. William son of Isaac Monday. p 83

4 January 1813. Francis MOODY and Joanna B. Earley. Sur. Jennings M. Jeffreys. Married 7 January by Rev. William Richards. p 496

11 February 1778. Archibald MOON and Martha Morton, dau. Josiah Morton who is surety. p 30

1 January 1811. Archibald MOON and Nancy Davis, dau. Samuel Davis who is surety. Married 3 January by Rev. Bernard Todd. p 475

18 September 1806. Josiah P. MOON and Elizabeth McKinney, dau. Charles McKinney. Sur. William McKinney. Married by Rev. Joshua worley. p 389

23 February 1803. William C. MOON and Unice Jones. Sur. Charles Harris. Married 3 March by Rev. Obadiah Edge. p 346

7 October 1799. George MOORE and Polly Alderson, dau. Mary Alderson. Sur. Joshua Foster. p 282

8 January 1801. Henry MOORE and Betsey Lester, dau. Morgan Lester who is surety. p 307

20 February 1788. Robert MOORE and Martha Hunter, consent of John Wilson who signs as father. Wit. to consent Alexander and John Hunter. Sur. Alexander Hunter. p 30

2 January 1786. Robert MOORE and Mary Barnes, dau. James Barnes, Sr. Sur. Francis Barnes. Married 1 February by Rev. John Williams. p 84

7 March 1805. Samuel MOORE and Sally Howard, dau. John Howard who is surety. Married 9 March by Rev. Joshua Worley. p 381

16 December 1815. Edmund MORGAN and Lucy Jackson, dau. Cain Jackson. Sur. Edmund Gaines. Married 21 December by Rev. John Chappell. p 530

29 October 1806. Dennis D. MORGAN and Frances Collier, ward of Langston Bacon. Sur. William Bacon. p 387

1 January 1813. Thomas MORGAN and Dorothy Williams, widow of Jeremiah Williams. Sur. John Carter. Married 13 January by Rev. Richard Dabbs. p 495

5 December 1796. Samuel MORGAN and Polly Hudson. Sur. Jacob Edwards. Married 24 December by Rev. William Dameron. p 238

23 February 1790. John MORRIS and Mary Elliott (widow). Sur. Richard Elliott. Married 24 February by Rev. William Mahon. p 144

3 July 1797. Joseph MORRIS and Anna Potter. Sur. Cain Jackson. Married same day by Rev. John Chappell. p 253

5 November 1787. Benjamin MORTON and Agnes Morton, dau. Thomas Morton, Gentleman. Sur. Thomas Read. p 109

8 November 1773. Charles MORTON and Mary Ann Smith. Sur. William Smith. p 21

19 December 1782. John MORTON and Martha Sampson. Married by Rev. John Weatherford. Ministers' Returns p 3

5 February 1814. John MORTON and Betsy Ann Le Grande, dau. Nash La Grande. Sur. Samuel Merry. p 513

4 January 1808. Meshack MORTON and Patsey Boulton. Sur. Hugh Frazier. p 414

13 June 1809. Richard MORTON and Martha Spencer, dau. Lucy Spencer. Sur. John D. Richardson. Married by Rev. Mathew Lyle. p 443

1 June 1795. Stephen MORTON and Selah Blankenship, dau. David Blankenship. Sur. Joseph Davis. p 225

29 December 1801. Thomas MORTON and Nancy Boulton, dau. John Boulton. Sur. Stephen Morton. Thomas son of John Morton. p 309

25 October 1798. William Lewis MORTON and Elizabeth Morton, dau. Quin Morton. Sur. William Morton. p 271

16 July 1788. Arthur MOSELEY and Nancy Bibbs, dau. John Bibbs. Sur. Richard Bouldin. Arthur son of Edward Moseley. Married 6 August by Rev. John Williams. p 123

29 May 1790. Edward MOSELEY, Jr. and Martha Dryson. Sur. John Norris. Married 2 June by Rev. John Williams. p 150

6 November 1809. Edward MOSELEY, Jr. and Becky Farrow Finch, ward of Thomas Finch. Sur. Richard Russell. Married 30 November by Rev. William Richards. p 444

5 September 1785. Hillery MOSELEY and Nancy Bedford, dau. Thomas Bedford, deceased, ward of James Hamlett (her brother-in-law). Sur. Richard Bouldin. Called Anne in her father's will. Married 11 October by Rev. Thomas Johnston. p 73

5 March 1792. Josiah MOSELEY and Elizabeth Bibb. Sur. Hillery Moseley. Married 14 March by Rev. John Williams. p 170

7 February 1803. Robert MOSELEY and Sophia Birthright, dau. Peter Birthright. Sur. Obadiah Belcher. Robert son of Edward Moseley. Married 10 February by Rev. Edward Almond. p 347

11 January 1809. William MOSELEY and Martha Bouldin, dau. Thomas Bouldin. Sur. Robert Mitchell. William son of Edward Moseley. Married 12 January by Rev. George Petty. p 439

26 September 1814. William MOSELEY and Rebecca Johnson, ward of Travis Brooks who is surety. Married 28 September by Rev. William Richards. p 517

5 June 1815. William F. MOSELEY and Unity Pamplin. Sur. Henry Moseley. p 530

4 October 1809. Joel MULLINS and Rebecca Cary, dau. John Cary. Sur. Edmund Mullens. p 444

29 July 1811. Reddick MULLINGS and Elizabeth Styene. Sur. Peter Mason. Reddick son of James Mullings. p 468

15 December 1797. George MULLINS and Nancy Collings, dau. Mary Collings. Sur. James Mullins. p 253

16 October 1798. James MULLINS and Amey Berkley, dau. Alexander Berkley. Sur. Thomas Green. p 271

3 December 1792. Jesse MULLINS and Anne Mullins. Sur. James Mullins. Married 5 December by Rev. Edward Almond. p 186

22 January 1805. James MURRELL and Obedience Rudd. Sur. William Atkins. Married 26 January by Rev. John Chappell. p 380

7 April 1808. Christian MYERS and Nancy Moore. Sur. Cadwallader Jones. Married 14 April by Rev. Richard Dabbs, Jr. p 414

12 December 1786. David MC CARGO and Nancy Portwood. Married by Rev. John Williams. See David McGeorge. Ministers' Returns p 7

30 December 1800. Hezekiah MC CARGO and Tabitha Herndon. Married by Rev. Edward Almond. Ministers' Returns p 26

8 May 1798. James MC CARGO and Prudence Roberts, dau. Martha Roberts. Sur. John Roberts. Married 22 May by Rev. Edward Almond. p 265

25 October 1806. John MC CARGO and Elizabeth W. Callicot, dau. James Callicot. Sur. Thomas McCargo. Married 29 October by Rev. Richard Dabbs, Jr. p 389

15 April 1796. Robert MC CARGO and Rebecca Portwood, dau. Elizabeth Portwood. Sur. Lloyd Portwood. Married 19 April by Rev. Edward Almond. p 238

31 December 1797. Dancy MC CRAW and Elizabeth Pugh, dau. Samuel Pugh. Dancy son of Stephen McCraw. p 263

2 January 1797. Daney MC CRAW and Elizabeth Pugh. Sur. John Pugh. Both marriages given. p 253

3 August 1813. James L. MC CRAW and Eliza B. Green, dau. Coleman Green. Sur. Hillery Moseley, Jr. Married 6 August by Rev. Thomas E. Jeter. p 511

21 December 1795. John Bryant MC CRAW and Massey Kennan, dau. Sarah Keenan. Sur. Luke Palmer. p 225

1 September 1804. Robert MC CUNE and Aggey Harboard. Sur. Pleasant Jennings. p 356

9 December 1786. David MC GEORGE and Nancy Portwood, dau. Thomas Portwood. Sur. Lloyd Portwood. See David McCargo. p 92

24 February 1794. John MC INDOE and Patsey Brown, dau. William Brown. Sur. Jeremiah Brown. Returned 10 April Court by Rev. John Chappell. p 215

6 November 1785. Morris MC KINNEY and Mary Fowler (widow). Sur. William Hames. Married 17 November by Rev. Thomas Johnston. p 72

25 January 1786. William MC KENNEY and Patsey Williamson. Married by Rev. John Weatherford. Ministers' Returns p 6

14 March 1814. John MC LEAN and Mary S. Armistead (widow). Sur. Benjamin Chapman. p 521

28 May 1785. Donald MC MICHAEL and Susannah Yuille. Married by Rev. Thomas Johnston. Ministers' Returns p 4

6 September 1802. William MC MICHAL and Elizabeth ugh, ward of Ezekiel Pugh who is surety. William son of John McMichal. Married 8 September by Rev. John Chappell. p 321

21 November 1788. John MC QUAY and Sally W. Goode, dau. Mackness Goode. Sur. Langston Bacon. p 124

3 December 1808. Levy NANCY and Judith E. Ligon. Sur. John Hord. p 417

26 May 1795. William NANCE and Martha Fulks. Sur. George Nevills. p 224

3 October 1808. Campbell NASH and Elizabeth Palmer, dau. Halcote Palmer who is surety. p 427

28 October 1806. James NASH and Jinsey Pugh, ward of Ezekial Pugh who is surety. Married 2 November by Rev. John Chappell who says _Jean_. p 386

26 August 1805. Robert NASH and Sabrey Redey. Sur. Thomas Moore. p 381

1 November 1784. Stephen NEAL and Lucy Haskins, dau. Thomas Haskins. Sur. Thomas Cox. Married 2 December by Rev. Thomas Johnston. p 61

5 July 1802. John NEIGHBORS and Jincy Elam, ward of Charles Raine. Sur. William Smith, Jr. John son of William Neighbors. Married same day by Rev. John Chappell. p 316

13 May 1815. John NEIGHBORS and Polly Smith. Married by Rev. John Chappell. Ministers' Returns p 43

7 August 1800. William NEIGHBORS and Elizabeth Elam. Married by Rev. John Chappell. Ministers' Returns p 25

12 September 1801. John NELSON and Polly Boulton, dau. John Boulton who is surety. Married 17 September by Rev. William Spencer. p 309

15 December 1797. James NEWCOMB and Frankey Hampton. Sur. Edward Hamblin. James son of John Newcomb. Married 21 December by Rev. Edward Almond. p 254

23 June 1803. Perry C. NOELL and Betsey Tatum. Sur. James Tatum. p 333

3 October 1808. William S. NORMAN and Peggy Barnes, dau. Francis Barnes who is surety. p 420

25 February 1799. Anthony NORTH and Fanny Holloway, dau. John Holloway. Sur. Peter Stem. p 282

13 May 1808. Francis NORTH and Elizabeth Branch, dau. Matthew Branch, Sr. of Prince Edward County. Sur. Anthony Womack. p 426

22 November 1796. Richard NORTH and Betty Davenport, dau. William Davenport. Sur. Charles McKinney. Married 25 November by Rev. Joshua McKinney. Married 25 November by Rev. Joshua Worley. p 238

6 October 1784. Thomas NORTH, Jr. and Mildred Overton (widow of James Overton). Sur. Valentine North. Married 16 October by Rev. John Weatherford. p 65

24 December 1796. Charles NORVEL and Susanna Dabbs. Married by Rev. Archibald Alexander. See Charles Nowell. Ministers' Returns p 21

24 December 1796. Charles NOWELL and Susannah Dabbs. Sur. William Dabbes. See Charles Norvel. p 239

28 December 1807. John NUCOMB and Susanna Wilmuth. Sur. Levi Brooks. Married 29 December by Rev. George Petty. p 404

25 November 1795. Clement OLD and Sally F. Goode, dau. Philip Goode. Sur. Dabney Collier. Married same day by Rev. Edward Almond. p 224

20 November 1811. Clement OLD and Fanny May. Sur. John Eubank. p 466

12 February 1805. Benjamin OLIVER and Rebecca Mason, dau. Charles
Mason. Sur. John Mason. Married 14 February by Rev. John Chappell.
p 367

2 November 1807. Charles OLIVER and Lucy Neal. Sur. Lewis Camp.
Married 26 November by Rev. William Richards. p 404

3 January 1796. David OLIVER and Elizabeth Armistead. Married by Rev.
William Mahon. Ministers' Returns p 19

13 November 1804. John OLIVER and Sally Armistead, dau. William
Armistead. Sur. John Armistead. Married 15 November by Rev. John
Chappell. p 351

2 April 1787. Joseph OLIVER and Catherine Griggs, dau. James Griggs.
Sur. Thomas Read. p 109

22 January 1810. Thomas OLIVER, Jr. and Anne Oliver, dau. John Oliver.
Sur. Edmund Patrick. Married 24 January by Rev. Richard Dabbs. p 452

4 July 1791. William OLIVER and Lucy Johnson. Sur. Philip Johnson.
p 156

21 October 1809. Claiborne OSBORNE and Judy Upton. Sur. Mitchell
Roberson. Married 26 October by Rev. George Petty. p 434

26 December 1798. Daniel OSBORNE and Patsey Collier, ward Langston
Bacon. Sur. Martin Williams. Married 27 December by Rev. Edward
Almond. p 265

24 December 1794. Edward OSBORNE and Sally Burchett. Sur. William
Burchett. Married 25 December by Rev. Edward Almond. p 220

4 September 1797. Philip OSBORNE and Betsey Gayle. Sur. Thomas Gayle.
Married 12 September by Rev. Edward Almond. p 255

6 January 1806. Reps. OSBORNE and Rebecca Goode, dau. Philip Goode who
is surety. Married 14 January by Rev. Richard Dabbs, Jr. p 386

7 August 1797. Thomas OSBORNE and Amy Gilliam, dau. Martha Gilliam.
Sur. John Gilliam. Married 10 August by Rev. Edward Almond. p 254

19 December 1815. William OSBORNE and Polly Osborne, dau. Samuel
Osborne. Sur. John Osborne. p 526

2 December 1811. Gideon N. OVERSTREET and Nancy Baldwin, dau. John
Baldwin. Sur. John Cage. Married 3 December by Rev. John Chappell
who says Fanny. p 468

21 May 1805. Sherwood L. OVERSTREET and Elizabeth Hazelwood, dau. John
Hazelwood. Sur. John Harris. Married 23 May by Rev. Bernard Todd.
p 381

2 December 1811. Thomas OVERSTREET and Patsey White. Sur. William
Overstreet. p 468

14 September 1775. James OVERTON and Mildred Clayton. Sur. John
Clayton. p 26

7 June 1813. John OVERTON and Polly Birthright, dau. Zachariah Birthright. Sur. Robert Moseley. p 496

3 January 1806. William OVERTON and Frankey Harvey, dau. William
Harvey. Sur. John C. Watkins. p 386

8 January 1792. Benjamin OWEN and Susanna Overton. Sur. Thomas Watts.
Benjamin son of James Owen. Married same day by Rev. Thomas
Dobson. p 174

7 March 1797. Peter PAGE and Elizabeth Wood, dau. E. Wood. Sur. Charles
Spencer. Married 18 March by Rev. Obadiah Edge. p 255

24 June 1779. Richard PAGE and Elizabeth Jones, dau. Richard Jones.
Sur. William Foster. p 33

1 September 1806. Coleman PALMER and Mary Lewis, dau. Benjamin Lewis
who is surety. Married 16 October by Rev. Edward Almond. p 385

5 October 1807. Daniel PALMER and Annis W. Palmer, dau. Chillion
Palmer who is surety. p 411

10 June 1807. Jeffrey PALMER, Jr. and Sally Palmer, widow of John
Palmer. Sur. Adam Mason. Jeffrey son of Jeffrey Palmer, Sr. p 411

11 February 1805. John PALMER and Sally Palmer, dau. Luke Palmer.
Sur. Aden Mason. p 368

12 March 1813. Laban PALMER and Catherine Lipscomb, dau. Richard
Lipscomb. Sur. Pleasant Lipscomb. p 494

18 November 1805. Le Grand PALMER and Susannah Palmer, dau. Luke
Palmer. Sur. Aden Mason. p 367

6 February 1809. Woodson PALMER and Delila Roberson, dau. John Roberson.
Sur. Benjamin Lewis. p 441

19 December 1814. Booker PALMOUR and Martha Mullings, dau. George
Mullings. Sur. Henry Mullings. Married same day by Rev. William
Fears. p 520

14 September 1790. Henry PAMPLIN and Esther Rice, dau. Thomas Rice.
Sur. Samuel Rice. p 149

20 December 1813. John PAMPLIN and Clarissa Pettus, dau. Thomas Pettus.
Sur. Martin Pettus. p 496

2 November 1802. Leonard PAMPLIN and Nancy Smith, ward of Presley
Bailey who is surety. Married 4 October by Rev. John Chappell.
p 318

23 March 1809. Richard PARKER and Nancy Bartee. Sur. John Bartee. p 440

5 October 1801. Martin PARKS and Nancy Goode. Sur. Gaines Goode.
Married 27 October by Rev. John Chappell. p 303

7 April 1806. William B. PARROW and Betsey R. North, dau. Anthony North. Sur. Thomas North. Married 22 April by Rev. Joshua Worley who says Patey. p 384

3 June 1793. Major PARSONS and Tabitha Hines, dau. Henry Hines. Sur. Thomas Parsons. Married 27 June by Rev. Joshua Worley. p 193

5 June 1786. Samuel PARSONS and Abigail Knowles, dau. Edward Knowles. Sur. Zachariah Maddox. p 91

3 December 1792. William PARSONS and Agnes Ramsey. Sur. John L. Ramsey. p 184

4 February 1793. William PARSONS and Mary Barklay, dau. Alexander Barklay. Sur. Charles McKinney. Married 8 February by Rev. John Weatherford. p 190

5 July 1784. James PATILLO and Rebecca Brown, dau. Russell Brown. Sur. Anthony North. p 65

12 March 1790. John V. PATILLO and Betsey Harroway, dau. Charles Harroway. Sur. James Patillo. Married 18 March by Rev. Joshua Worley. p 146

17 August 1799. Robert PATILLO and Mary Ann Hayes, dau. Richard Hayes. Sur. Grief Barksdale. p 283½

27 January 1794. Edmund PATRICK and Nancy Oliver, dau. Thomas Oliver. Sur. John Patrick. p 216

3 November 1788. John PATRICK and Sally Moseley, dau. Edward Moseley. Sur. James Bryant. Married 13 November by Rev. John Williams. p 112

19 May 1803. Harvey PAULETT and Betsey Harvey, dau. William Harvey. Sur. Thomas Harvey. Married 24 May by Rev. Joshua Worley. p 345

7 March 1803. Richard PAULETT and Frances Richardson, dau. John Richardson. Sur. John P. Richardson. Married 17 March by Rev. Joshua Worley. p 345

5 October 1789. William PAYLOR and Nancy Scott, dau. Thomas Scott. Sur. James Patillo. Married 8 October by Rev. John Weatherford. p 129

4 May 1790. Thomas PAYNE and Nancy Price, dau. William Price. Sur. William Price, Jr. Married 20 May by Rev. William Mahon. p 146

18 November 1795. Martin PEARCE and Judith Spencer. Sur. John Spencer. Married 26 November by Rev. Archibald Alexander. p 227

1 July 1806. John B. PEARSON and Margaret Rawlins, dau. John Rawlins. Sur. Thomas Lee. Married 2 July by Rev. James Elmore. p 385

20 May 1788. Joseph PEARSON and Jeane Lee, dau. John Lee. Sur. Robert Bedford. Married by Rev. David Ellington. p 120

25 June 1787. William PEDLAR and Sally Chisholm. Married by Rev. John Weatherford. Ministers' Returns p 8

30 July 1792. William PEGG and Magdalen Blankenship, dau. David Blankenship. Sur. Abel Blankenship. p 180

31 January 1797. John PENN and Phoebe Cayse. Sur. Jesse Adams. p 256

11 January 1797. Freeman PENTICOST and Jincy Fleming, dau. William Fleming. Sur. William Lane. Married 12 January by Rev. Thomas Dobson. p 255

10 July 1802. John PENTICOST and Elizabeth Pamplin, dau. Henry and Esther Pamplin. Sur. Paschal Tucker. Married same day by Rev. John Chappell. p 317

25 January 1806. Richard PENTICOST and Amy Sullivant, ward of Griffin Dodd who is surety. p 385

7 January 1800. Scarborough PENTICOST and Polly Pamplin. Married by Rev. John Chappell. Ministers' Returns p 24

5 December 1785. William PENTICOST and Lucy Johns (widow). Sur. Hubbard Williams. Married 14 January 1786, by Rev. John Weatherford. p 75

10 November 1808. William PENTICOST and Biddy Mann, dau. Jesse Mann who is surety. Married same day by Rev. George Petty who says Obedy (Obedience?). p 417

21 October 1790. Harlow (Arbord) PERKINSON and Susanna Brooks, dau. Joel and Betty Brooks. Sur. Jesse Mann. p 149

7 November 1814. Hubert PERKINSON and Priscilla Petty, dau. John Petty. Sur. George Petty. p 521

31 October 1808. Jackman PERKINSON and Elizabeth Rice, widow of John Rice. Sur. Patrick Connally. Married 1 November by Rev. William Fears. p 417

11 April 1814. John D. PERKINSON and Polly Hundley, dau. John Hundley. Sur. Coleman Perkinson. Married same day by Rev. George Petty. p 521

19 December 1795. Page PERKINSON and Peggy Monday, sister of William Monday who is surety. Married 21 December by Rev. Edward Almond. p 224

26 October 1787. Seth PERKERSON and Tabitha Gill. Married by Rev. John Williams. Ministers' Returns p 8

9 February 1789. Elisha PERKINS and Elizabeth Watkins, dau. William Watkins. Sur. Daniel White. Married 20 February by Rev. John Weatherford. p 131

14 January 1809. Anthony PERRIMAN and Elizabeth E. Adams, dau. Thomas Adams who is surety. Married 19 January by Bernard Todd. p 441

4 March 1802. Freeman PETTUS and Susanna Pettus. Married by Rev. Edward Almond. Ministers' Returns p 28

2 January 1800. John PETTUS and Susanna Neale. Married by Rev. Edward Almond. Ministers' Returns p 25

3 December 1783. Thomas PETTUS and Polly Madison, dau. Henry Madison. Sur. Thomas Gaines. Married 9 December by Rev. Thomas Johnston. p 59

7 December 1807. William PETTUS and Elizabeth Patrick, dau. John Patrick. Sur. Freeman Pettus. Married 23 December by Rev. John Chappell. p 406

27 December 1797. Andy PETTY and Martha Farmer. Sur. Stephen Farmer. Andy son of Davis Petty. Married 3 January 1798, by Rev. Edward Almond. p 256

23 December 1799. George PETTY and Susannah Brizendine, dau. Isaac and Anne Brizendine. Sur. Joshua Brizendine. Married 26 December by Rev. Edward Almond. p 283

23 January 1815. James PETTY and Lucinda Williams, dau. Mastin Williams. Sur. Daniel Petty. p 524

30 November 1799. John PETTY, Jr. and Elizabeth Fears, dau. William Fears. Sur. George Petty. John son of John Petty, Sr. Married 5 December by Rev. William Richards. p 283

11 January 1802. Thomas PETTY and Susanna Gill, dau. Michael Gill who is surety. Married 14 January by Rev. William Richards. p 317

16 December 1807. William PHAMP and Polly Morgan, dau. John Morgan who is surety. Married same day by Rev. Richard Dabbs, Jr. p 411

30 November 1789. John PHARIS and May Key. Married by Rev. John Weatherford. Ministers' Returns p 11

12 May 1801. James PHILLIPS and Milly Penticost, dau. William Penticost. Sur. Scarborough Penticost. James son of Anthony Phillips. Married 13 May by Rev. Obadiah Edge. p 303

5 January 1807. James PHILLIPS and Nancy Jackson, ward of Elijah Clark who is surety. Married 8 January by Rev. John Fore. p 410

7 May 1792. John PHILIPS and Sarah Parsons, dau. Thomas Parsons. Sur. Anthony Philips. p 173

16 August 1809. Abiezer PLUMMER and Polly Hudson, dau. Daniel Hudson. Sur. John Plummer. Married 17 August by Rev. Hezekiah McLelland. p 433

15 February 1793. Thomas C. POAGE and Jeane Watkins. Sur. Henry A. Watkins. Married 19 February by Rev. Drury Lacy. p 191

7 November 1791. George POLLARD and Mary Crews, dau. William Crews. Sur. William Morton   Married 17 November by Rev. Thomas Dobson. p 166

13 March 1811. Jesse POLLARD and Julia Weatherford, dau. Stephen Weatherford. Sur. John Pollard. Jesse son of George Pollard. p 470

26 June 1801. Samuel POLLARD and Sally Mullins, dau. William Mullins who is surety. p 303

21 March 1815. Warner POLLARD and Barbara Haley, dau. John Haley. Sur. Archibald Haley. p 524

12 September 1805. John POLLOCK and Elizabeth Petty, dau. John Petty. Sur. Matthias Petty. Married 14 September by Rev. William Richards. p 367

4 June 1813. Lewis D. POINDEXTER and Nancy Smith, dau. Isaac Smith. Sur. Thomas B. Smith. p 504

6 March 1809. Richard POINDEXTER and Mourning Ford, dau. Ezekiel Ford. Sur. Thomas Adams. p 441

3 January 1785. John PORTER and Sarah Clark, dau. John Clark. Sur. Thomas Clark. Married 2 February by Rev. John Weatherford. p 75

6 October 1783. Oliver PORTER and Margaret Watson, dau. Douglas Watson. Sur. William Porter. p 57

18 August 1790. Samuel PORTER and Ursula Farguson, widow of John Farguson. Sur. Jordan Sublett. Samuel Porter of Prince Edward County. Married 19 August by Rev. Joshua Worley. p 138

8 January 1799. Lloyd PORTWOOD and Polly Sullivant. Married by Rev. John Ligon. Ministers' Returns p 23

17 October 1796. Robert PORTWOOD and Mary Ferrell Newton, dau. Giles Newton. Married 27 October by Rev. Edward Almond who says Mary Terrill Newton. p 239

7 January 1799. Robert PORTWOOD and Nancy Burrow, ward of Moses Harrison. Sur. Samuel Martin. Married 8 January by Rev. John Ligon. p 283

22 December 1792. Thomas PORTWOOD and Elizabeth McCargo, dau. John McCargo. Sur. Robert McCargo. Married 27 December by Rev. John Williams. p 174

16 September 1806. Thomas PORTWOOD and Milley Hall, ward of John Purnell. Sur. John Brizendine. p 384

19 February 1813. Branch POWELL and Armin Burchett, dau. William Burchett. Sur. Edmund Duffer. p 493

7 February 1803. James POWELL and Nancy Bottom, dau. Miles Bottom who is surety. See James Howell. p 336

2 December 1793. Nathaniel PRICE and Polly Venable. Sur. George Lyon. Married 18 December by Rev. Drury Lacy. p 191

11 February 1807. Robert PRICE and Fannie S. Chappell, dau. John Chappell. Sur. Thomas E. Jeter. p 410

12 October 1771. William PRICE and Mary Gaines, dau. Richard Gaines who is surety. p 10

1 March 1790. William PRICE and Caty Gaines, dau. Richard Gaines. Sur. William Gaines. Married 11 March by Rev. William Mahon. p 147

15 November 1797. William PRICE and Polly Richardson. Married by Rev. Joshua Worley. Ministers' Returns p 22

19 February 1801. William PRICE and Hannah Fuqua. Married by Rev. John Chappell. Ministers' Returns p 26

25 December 1804. William PRITCHARD and Nancy Elliott. Married by Rev. Mathew Dance. See William Pritchett. Ministers' Returns p 31

25 December 1804. William PRITCHETT and Nancy Elliott, dau. William Elliott. Sur. Clememnt R. Jameson. See William Pritchard. p 357

2 April 1787. Samuel PRYOR and Mary Wimbish, dau. Benjamin Wimbish. Sur. James Wimbish. p 109

2 August 1802. Samuel PRYOR and Sally Stembridge, dau. John Stembridge who is surety. p 318

24 November 1810. John PUCKETT and Elizabeth Hines, dau. Henry Hines. Sur. James Hines. Married 25 November by Rev. Joshua Worley. p 450

17 December 1803. Abraham PUGH and Anna Totty. Sur. Caldwell Wood. Married 21 December by Rev. John Chappell. p 339

19 December 1805. Ezekiel PUGH and Susanna Thomas. Sur. John Pugh. Married 26 December by Rev. John Chappell. p 368

29 June 1809. John M. PUGH and Sarah George, dau. Thomas George. Sur. William George. Married by Rev. Mathew Lyle. p 442

11 January 1813. John PUGH and Peggy Dabbs, dau. Joseph Dabbs. Sur. Richard Dabbs. Married 19 January by Rev. Richard Dabbs. p 494

16 December 1785. Samuel PUGH and Elizabeth Thomas, dau. Philip Thomas. Sur. William George. Married by Rev. Thomas Johnston who says 21 November. p 81

2 March 1795. Young PUGH and Peggy Parsons. Sur. Ezekiel Pugh. Married same day by Rev. Obadiah Edge. p 227

7 June 1790. Joseph PULLIAM and Mary Parsons, dau. William Parsons. Sur. William Marshall. p 145

1 January 1789. Seth PURKESON and Mary Vaughan (widow). Sur. William Wallding. Married 3 January by Rev. John Williams. p 128

3 September 1770. Sherwood PURSON and Elizabeth Ligon, dau. Thomas Ligon. p 8

5 December 1784. Lipscomb RAGLAND and Martha Watkins, dau. John Watkins who is surety. Married same day by Rev. Thomas Johnston. p 64

4 September 1786. Noah RAILEY and Elizabeth Harris, dau. Hanna Harris. Sur. John Sandifer. p 96

19 July 1777. Robert RAKESTRAW and Mary Grigg (widow). Sur. William
Price. p 28

13 March 1800. John RAMSEY and Martha Pugh. Married by Rev. John
Chappell. Ministers' Returns p 24

11 October 1806. John RAMSEY and Nancy Hazelwood, dau. Benjamin
Hazelwood. Sur. Sherwood L. Overstreet. Married 12 October by Rev.
John Chappell. p 382

2 March 1795. Joseph RAMSEY and Sally Pugh. Sur. William Parsons.
Married 5 March by Rev. Obadiah Edge. p 231

7 November 1796. William RAMSEY and Polly Pugh. Sur. John S. Ramsey.
Married 10 November by Rev. John Chappell. p 240

3 October 1785. Michael RANDALL and Peggy Adams, dau. James Adams.
Sur. Jeremiah Bonner. Married 24 October by Rev. John Weatherford.
p 75

7 November 1785. James RATHER and Elizabeth Rowton, dau. William
Rowton who is surety. Married 10 November by Rev. Thomas Johnston.
p 74

19 June 1781. John RAWLINS and Neff Terrill. Sur. William Rawlins. p 43

7 October 1799. Skipwith RAY and Polly Hutcheson, dau. Matthew Hutcheson.
Sur. William Hutcheson. p 279

27 March 1786. John Nash READ and Elizabeth Julia Spencer, ward of
Thomas Spencer, Jr. Sur. Thomas Read. Married 28 March by Rev.
Thomas Johnston. p 93

10 February 1790. Thomas READ, Jr. and Anna Haskins, dau. Thomas
Haskins. Sur. Thomas Read. p 152

17 September 1786. William READ and Elizabeth Bryant. Sur. Levy
Blankenship. p 121

2 December 1802. William READ and Patience Sims. Married by Rev.
Obadiah Edge. Ministers' Returns p 28

23 December 1796. Hugh REASE and Lucy Campbell, dau. John Campbell.
Sur. Joseph Rease. See Hugh Reese. p 241

7 August 1786. John REDDING and Elender Philby (orphan). John son of
George Redding. Sur. John Weatherford. p 91

15 May 1787. Robert REDDING and Mary Harrison Leason. Married by Rev.
John Weatherford. Ministers' Returns p 8

9 September 1809. Collier REDMAN and Nancy Haley, dau. Susanna Haley.
Sur. Archibald Haley. Married 14 September by Rev. George Petty.
p 429

17 December 1814. George REDMAN and Kissee Foard, dau. John Foard.
Sur. John Redman. p 520

2 October 1809. Thomas REDMAN and Susannah Traynum. Sur. Matthew Williams. Married 3 October by Rev. Joseph Jenkins. p 430

8 June 1774. William REDMAN and Polly Gouge (widow). Sur. Mack Hamblin. p 25

8 November 1804. George REDMON and Nancy Brizendine. Sur. Benjamin Laine. Married 9 November by Rev. Edward Almond. p 363

30 May 1789. Herod REESE and Judith Weaver. Married by Rev. John Weatherford. Ministers' Returns p 11

29 December 1796. Hugh REESE and Lucretia Chappell. Married by Rev. William Dameron. See Hugh Rease. Ministers' Returns p 21

19 May 1800. James REESE and Anne Ward (widow). Sur. John Spencer. Married 22 May by Rev. John Chappell. p 299

23 May 1814. Theodore REID and Sallie B. Harvey, dau. Nathan Harvey. Sur. Benjamin Marshall. p 519

9 January 1796. George REVELEY and Judith Sydnor Jennings, dau. Robert Jennings. Sur. Jack S. Davenport. George Reverley of Campbell County. See George Beverly. p 240

10 November 1800. David Allegree REYNOLDS and Polly Wheeler, dau. John Wheeler, Sr. Sur. Charles McKinney. Married by Rev. Bernard Todd. p 298

25 January 1794. James REYNOLDS and Nancy Prewit, dau. James Prewit. Sur. James Adams. Married 30 January by Rev. Henry Lester who says Prewitt. p 216

2 September 1815. John REYNOLDS and Polly Adams, dau. William Adams. Sur. Joseph Reynolds. p 525

28 January 1781. Joseph REYNOLDS and Massey Maddox, dau. Wilson Maddox. Sur. James Adams. p 42

2 January 1797. David RICE and Sally Johns. Sur. William Rice. Married 19 January by Rev. William Dameron. p 257

6 January 1795. James RICE and Rebecca Brooke, dau. Dudley Brooke. Sur. Zachariah Brooke. Married same day by Rev. Edward Almond. p 227

24 October 1792. John RICE and Anna Johns. Sur. Thomas Johns. Consent for John Rice by William Penticost. Married 26 October by Rev. William Hill. p 180

20 December 1815. Samuel RICE and Frances Kersey. Sur. Thomas Kersey. p 527

7 October 1812. Thomas RICE and Sally Jackson, dau. Thomas Jackson who is surety. p 477

15 July 1786. William RICE and Sally Parker McCraw, dau. Stephen McCraw. Sur. Thomas Read. p 95

2 November 1796. Isham RICHARDSON and Lucy Thornton. Sur. Francis Thornton. Married 24 November by Rev. Joshua Worley. p 240

16 July 1806. Isham RICHARDSON and Polly B. Harvey, dau. William Harvey. Sur. John C. Watkins. Married 17 July by Rev. Joshua Worley. p 383

29 November 1808. James RICHARDSON and Mary Watkins, dau. George Watkins. Sur. William Watkins. Married by Rev. Mathew Lyle. p 416

2 May 1803. John D. RICHARDSON and Elizabeth Spencer, dau. Thomas Spencer who is surety. p 340

1 June 1801. William RICHARDSON and Milly Jordan, dau. Matthew Jordan who is surety. Married 11 June by Rev. Joshua Worley. p 305

1 November 1802. William RICHARDSON and Patty Jackson, dau. Cain Jackson who is surety. p 318

19 April 1809. Howard L. RIDLEY and Mildred Sims (widow). Sur. Joseph Morton. Married 20 April by Rev. John H. Rice who says Howell L. Ridley. p 430

7 January 1803. Elisha ROACH and Barbara Tenor, dau. Daniel Tenor who is surety. Elisha son of John Roach, Sr. p 341

13 June 1793. Isaac ROACH and Susanna Shasteen, dau. John Shasteen (Chastain?). Sur. John Roach, Jr. Isaac son of John Roach, Sr. Married 18 June by Rev. Henry Lester. p 199

5 December 1796. John ROACH and Patsey Williamson. Sur. Daniel Williamson. Married 7 December by Rev. John Chappell. p 239

2 December 1805. Joshua ROACH and Elizabeth Johnston, dau. James Johnston. Sur. William Johnston. Married 26 December by Rev. Richard Dabbs, Jr. p 368

17 November 1810. Price ROACH and Catherine H. Gaines, dau. Thomas Gaines. Sur. John Miller. Married 22 November by Rev. Richard Dabbs. p 448

8 April 1809. William ROACH, Jr. and Jennie Brizendine, dau. Reuben Brizendine who is surety. p 443

7 February 1814. Fayette ROAN and Elizabeth H. Hunt, ward of Christopher Hunt. Sur. Samuel Merry. p 519

27 January 1788. Holcombe ROBERSON and Ruth Johnston, dau. Samuel Johnston. Sur. William Johnston. Married by Rev. John Weatherford who says 12 January, p 122

8 April 1815. James ROBERSON and Elizabeth Munday. Sur. Levi Brooks. p 527

26 December 1800. Bartlett ROBERTS and Rebecca M. Fears. Married by Rev. Edward Almond. Ministers' Returns p 26

27 November 1799. Benjamin ROBERTS and Judith Fuqua. Married by Rev. Edward Almond. Ministers' Returns p 25

18 April 1808. Benjamin ROBERTS and Nancy Fuqua. Sur. Richard Carter. Married 20 April by Rev. Mathew Dance. p 423

7 June 1785. Daniel ROBERTS and Margaret Purcell. Married by Rev. Thomas Johnston. Ministers' Returns p 4

6 October 1797. Francis ROBERTS and Jane Herndon, dau. Joseph Herndon. Sur. John Roberts. Married 9 February (?) by Rev. Edward Almond who says Jean. p 256

20 December 1791. Henry ROBERTS and Aney May, dau. Edmund May. Sur. Claiborne Osborne. Married 26 December by Rev. John Williams who says Amy May. p 163

5 August 1793. John ROBERTS and Lewsany Petty, dau. John Petty. Sur. Thomas Petty. Married 8 August by Rev. Thomas Dobson. p 200

11 November 1783. Robert ROBERTS and Susannah Haley. Married by Rev. Thomas Johnston. Ministers' Returns p 1

21 March 1807. Samuel ROBERTS and Sally Stowe, dau. William and Clary Stowe. Sur. Elisah Smith. Married by Rev. John Chappell. p 410

3 January 1787. Simon ROBERTS and Nancy Bowman, dau. Royall Bowman. Sur. Robert Bowman. Married by Rev. Thomas Johnston who says 5 July. p 104

22 December 1788. Thomas ROBERTS and Nancy May, dau. Daniel and Alsey May. Sur. John May. Married 24 December by Rev. John Williams. p 121

7 March 1803. Thomas ROBERTS and Sallie Herndon, dau. Joseph Herndon. Sur. Francis Roberts. Married 10 March by Rev. Edward Almond. p 341

6 November 1789. William ROBERTS and Nancy Toombs, dau. Hansey Toombs. Sur. Jesse Roberson. Married 10 November by Rev. John Williams. p 136

22 December 1791. Brooks ROBERTSON and Rhoda Callicot, dau. James Callicot. Brooks son of Henry Robertson, Sr. who is surety. Married 23 December by Rev. John Williams. p 161

23 December 1809. Christopher ROBERTSON and Francis C. Cayse, dau. Pleasant Cayse. Sur. John Johnson. Married 26 December by Rev. Mathew Lyle. p 440

3 April 1793. David ROBERTSON and Nancy Callicot, dau. James Callicot. Sur. Brooks Robertson. Married 12 April by Rev. John Williams. p 201

14 October 1808. Henry ROBERTSON and Martha B. Crenshaw. Sur. Lyddall Bacon. Married 18 October by Rev. David McCargo. p 426

21 January 1774. James ROBERTSON and Sarah Solkins Nancy, dau. Frederick Nance who is surety. James son of Nathaniel Robertson. James Robertson son of Amelia County. p 25

2 June 1794. John ROBERTSON and Molly Cook Bailey. Sur. David Bailey. p 217

25 December 1804. Mitchell ROBERTSON and Sally Upton, dau Lucy Upton. Sur. John Rutledge. Married 27 December by Rev. Edward Almond. p 357

30 August 1806. Nathaniel ROBERTSON and Nancy Williamson, dau. Jacob Williamson. Sur. Levi Brooks. Married 4 September by Rev. James Elmore. p 382

16 October 1797. William ROBERTSON and Susannah Moseley, dau. Edward Moseley, Jr. Sur. Brooks Robertson. Married 19 October by Rev. William Richards. p 257

21 December 1797. William ROBERTSON and Mary N. Lawton. Sur. Robert Lawton. p 257

1 December 1794. Robert ROBESON and Salley Johnston. Sur. James Johnston. Married 25 December by Rev. John Weatherford. p 127

11 March 1789. Elias ROBEY and Mary Carter, dau. George Carter. Sur. Silas Johnson. Married 15 March by Rev. Thomas Johnston. p 128

5 December 1808. James ROBEY and Jincy Weatherford, dau. Stephen Weatherford. Sur. Eli Robey. Married 8 December by Rev. Richard Dabbs. p 416

30 December 1802. Thomas ROBINSON and Martha White, dau. William White. Sur. John White. p 319

7 November 1791. James RODGERS and Ann Phelps. Sur. John Phelps. p 156

13 November 1805. William ROFFE and Rebecca Rice, widow of James Rice. Sur. George Petty. p 369

2 July 1787. Ezekiel ROGERS and Rebecca Williamson, dau. Cuthbert Williamson. Sur. James Patillo. Married 5 July by Rev. John Weatherford. p 104

16 July 1791. Nathaniel ROGERS and Catharine Brent, dau. John Brent. Sur. James Moon. p 159

23 May 1805. Philip R. ROOTES and Elizabeth Smith, dau. Thomas Smith. Sur. William Smith. p 369

25 December 1788. Peter ROSS and Lucy Carwiles, dau. William Carwiles. Sur. Charles McKenney. p 121

16 February 1810. John ROWTON and Martha Ferguson, dau. Francis Ferguson. Sur. John Wyatt. p 446

28 October 1806. William ROWTON, Jr. and Sarah D. Adams, dau. Charles Adams. Sur. Stephen Stowell. Married 29 October by Rev. Bernard Todd. p 383

22 May 1806. Willis ROWTON and Mary Scott, dau. Thomas Scott. Sur. Charles Spencer. Married same day by Rev. Bernard Todd. p 383

24 January 1787. William ROYALL and Betsey Flippen Bedford. Sur. Robert Bedford. Married by Rev. Thomas Johnston who says 24 July. p 103

21 December 1803. Thomas RUDD and Catherine White, dau. Matthew and Martha White. Sur. Charles Williamson. p 344

23 December 1793. Samuel RUDDER and Rebecca Brown. Sur. Burwell Brown. Married 24 December by Rev. Thomas Dobson. p 201

25 January 1785. Burnel (or Burnet) RUSSELL and Prudence Hogan. Married by Rev. Thomas Johnston. Ministers' Returns p 5

1 January 1810. Hezekiah RUSSELL and Elizabeth Featherstone. Sur. Snelling Wilkerson. Married same day by Rev. William Fears. p 449

1 February 1808. Richard RUSSELL and Polly Moseley, dau. Hillery Moseley who is surety. Married 7 February by Rev. William Richards. p 426

26 September 1774. William RUSSELL and Anne Ferguson. Sur. Thomas Read. p 24

9 November 1815. David RUTLEDGE and Synthy Hundley, dau. John Hundley. Sur. Richard Rutledge. Married same day by Rev. George Petty. p 525

11 January 1794. John RUTLEDGE and Sally Logins. Married by Rev. Thomas Dobson. Ministers' Returns p 17

4 January 1799. Richard RUTLEDGE and Jenny Milam. Sur. John Rutledge. Married 10 January by Rev. Edward Almond. p 275

20 January 1808. Richard RUTLEDGE and Mary Newcomb, dau. John Newcomb. Sur. David Rutledge. Married same day by Rev. George Petty. p 416

1 July 1809. Thomas RUTLEDGE and Betsey Going, dau. Thomas Going. Sur. James Brooke. Married 2 July by Rev. Richard Dabbs. p 439

13 August 1804. William RUTLEDGE and Polly Hamblin. Sur. John Rutledge. Married 14 August by Rev. Edward Almond. p 358

9 June 1794. David RYAN and Nancy Roach. Sur. William Roach. Married 10 June by Rev. Joshua Worley. p 216

6 February 1811. Randolph RYAN and Sally Osborne, dau. Leticia Williamson. Sur. Thomas Roberts. Married 7 February by Rev. George Petty. p 465

28 December 1797. William RYAN, Jr. and Sarah Adkins, dau. John and Esther Adkins. Sur. William Adkins. William Ryan son of William Rion. p 246

22 February 1800. William RYAN and Gilley Lunnon. Sur. Thomas Blanks. Married 25 February by Rev. Edward Almond who says Lonnon. p 298

24 August 1799. Francis RYON and Patty Maddox, dau. David Maddox. Sur. Michael Maddox. Married 29 August by Rev. John Chappell. p 275

6 May 1793. William SALMON and Betty Page (widow). Sur. William Stembridge. Married same day by Rev. Edward Almond. p 197

3 February 1773. James SANDERSON and Martha Worsham. Sur. Benjamin
Breedlove. p 19

25 May 1796. William SCATES and Mary Kersy, dau. Lucy Kersy. Sur.
Martell Luvern. Willliam Scates of Halifax County. p 237

5 July 1813. Zachariah SCATES and Unisa Martin, dau. John Martin.
Sur. William Stowe. p 493

17 December 1790. Charles SCOTT and Priscilla Read. Sur. Clement Read.
Married 22 December by Rev. Archibald McRobert. p 149

15 March 1808. William SCOTT and Pauline Daniel, ward of Charlie
Daniel. Sur. Henry Embry Scott. p 421

1 October 1814. William M. SCOTT and Nancy Daniel. Sur. Stephen Bedford. p 518

5 December 1796. James SHARRER and Mary Thompson. Married by Rev.
Obadiah Edge. (Probably date of return.) See James Shearn.
Ministers' Returns p 20

27 December 1804. Hugh SHAW and Elizabeth Woodson Morton, dau. Little
Joe Morton. Sur. William Morton. Married 28 December by Rev. John
H. Rice. p 364

27 February 1792. Peter SHEARHAM and Mary Williams, dau. Ann Loggins.
Sur. Matthew Williams. Married 1 March by Rev. John Williams. p 180

17 August 1796. James SHEARN and Mary Thompson (widow). Sur. John
Harvey. See James Sharrer. p 237

15 September 1782. Peter SHEERMAN and Ruhamour Jones. Married by Rev.
Thomas Johnston. Ministers' Returns p 2

28 January 1791. Absalom SHELTON and Polly Clements, dau. Benjamin
Clements. Sur. Josiah Foster. Absalom brother of Godfrey Shelton.
Married 29 January by Rev. Edward Almond. p 165

2 February 1788. Godfrey SHELTON and Molly Williams, dau. Thomas
Williams. Sur. Thomas Bedford. Married 7 February by Rev. Thomas
Johnston. p 125

4 June 1792. Stephen SHELTON and Sinah Breedlove. Sur. James Breedlove.
p 178

28 August 1806. Benjamin SHORT and Susanna Jones. Married by Rev.
Richard Dabbs, Jr. Ministers' Returns p 34

2 August 1802. Berry SHORTER and Siney Stembridge, dau. John Stembridge
who is surety. p 320

16 April 1810. Jeremiah SHORTER and Betsey Hamlett, dau. William
Hamlett who is surety. Married 19 April by Rev. John Chappell. p 460

9 December 1806. John SHORTER and Nancy Palmore (Palmer). Sur. Benjamin Lewis. John son of James Shorter. Married 11 December by Rev.
Edward Almond. p 391

27 June 1799. Robert SHORTER and Sally Kennady, dau. John Kennady.
Sur. James Shorter. p 276

25 October 1789. Amos SILCOCK and Clary Mason. Married by Rev. John
Weatherford. Ministers' Returns p 12

2 May 1786. Richard SILCOCK and Bashty Arnold, dau. James Arnold. Sur.
David Eudaly. Married same day by Rev. Thomas Johnston who says
Vastile. (Probably Vashti). p 95

1 August 1774. John SIMMONS and Keturah King Mary Ann Stegar. Sur.
William Simmons. p 22

5 December 1798. John SIMMONS and Sally Hundley Matthews, dau. Kincey
Matthews. Sur. Edward Hamilton. Married 6 December by Rev. Edward
Almond. p 264

19 December 1808. Randolph SIMMONS and Nancy Eanes, dau. Arthur Eans
who is surety. Married 22 September by Rev. John Chappell. p 422

3 January 1774. David SIMMS and Letty May. Sur. Mackness Goode. p 25

7 August 1790. John SIMMS and Martha Bartee, dau. Pheby Bartee. Sur.
David Bartee, brother. Married 9 September by Rev. William Mahon.
p 148

7 March 1774. Matthew SIMS and Amey May, dau. Gabriel May who is surety.
p 23

18 April 1785. James SKELTON and Mary Mullins. Sur. Abner May. p 74

17 September 1811. Charles H. Slaughter and Polly Anderson, dau.
Charles Anderson. Sur. James Wheeler. Married 19 September by Rev.
John Chappell. p 464

16 December 1808. David SLAUGHTER and Anne Newcomb, dau. John Newcomb
who is surety. p 421

6 June 1805. John SLAUGHTER and Martha Armistead, dau. William Armistead,
Sr. who is surety. Married 11 June by Rev. John Chappell. p 378

23 November 1786. Richard SLYATH and Mary Childress, dau. Jeremiah
Childress. Sur. Richard Page. See Richard Slythe. p 88

22 November 1786. Richard SLYTHE and Mary Childress. Married by Rev.
Thomas Johnston. See Richard Slyath. Ministers' Returns p 7

4 November 1805. Robert SMALLMAN and Martha Cheatham, dau. Benjamin
Cheatham. Sur. Joseph Cheatham. Married 20 November by Rev.
Richard Dabbs, Jr. p 378

5 March 1789. Benoni SMITH and Mildred Vaughan, dau. Abraham Vaughan.
Sur. Thomas Read. Married same day by Rev. Thomas Johnston. p 132

19 April 1810. Benoni SMITH and Polly Barley. Sur. Samuel Barley.
Married 20 April by Rev. John Chappell. p 447

15 March 1806. Elisha SMITH and Patsey Cumbee, dau. Thomas Cumbee. Sur. William Turner. Married 27 March by Rev. Richard Dabbs, Jr. p 391

11 October 1770. Isaac SMITH and Lucy Wright, dau. W. Wright. Sur. Joseph Moore. p 9

6 October 1784. Isaac SMITH and Sarah Hancock, dau. Anthony Hancock who is surety. Married 9 December by Rev. Thomas Johnston. p 62

22 December 1807. Isaac SMITH and Betsey Woodfin, dau. George Woodfin. Sur. William Smith. Married 24 December by Rev. Richard Dabbs, Jr. p 406

1 May 1780. John SMITH and Jeane Brent, dau. John Brent who is surety. p 39

31 October 1796. John SMITH and Polly Galimore, dau. William Galimore. Sur. Thomas Hayse. Married 3 November by Rev. Edward Almond. p 237

15 November 1796. John SMITH and Susannah Harvey (widow). Sur. Simon Jackson. Married 17 November by Rev. John Chappell who says Susannah Haney. p 242

2 September 1799. John SMITH and Sally Atkins, dau. Joseph Atkins who is surety. p 277

29 October 1806. John SMITH and Jinsey Hendrick, dau. Daniel Hendrick who is surety. Married same day by Rev. James Elmore. p 391

5 November 1810. Owen SMITH and Susanna Woodfin, dau. George Woodfin. Sur. John Woodfin. Married 15 October (?) by Rev. John Chappell. p 447

17 February 1804. Reuben SMITH and Elizabeth Garrett, dau. Francis Garrett. Sur. John Davis. p 359

18 January 1785. Stephen SMITH, Jr. and Lettice Mullins, dau. James and Mary Mullins. Sur. Owen Sullivant. Married 20 January by Rev. Thomas Johnston. p 74

4 October 1784. Thomas SMITH and Molly Fuqua, dau. Joseph Fuqua. Sur. Paschall Greenhill. Married 4 November by Rev. Thomas Johnston. p 63

27 June 1803. Thomas SMITH, Jr. and Milly Rosser. Sur. Charles Raine. Thomas son of Thomas Smith, Sr. p 344

7 May 1798. William SMITH and Ann Dickerson. Sur. William Hames. Married 18 May by Rev. Edward Almond. p 264

6 January 1812. Richard SMITHSON and Polly B. Cox, dau. Thomas Cox. Sur. William Towler. Richard Smithson of Lunenburg County. p 480

5 November 1794. Pleasant SNEAD and Petsey A. Foster. Sur. John Foster. p 217

29 October 1799. George SORVELL and Polly S. Hames. Married by Rev. Joshua Worley. Ministers' Returns p 24

13 December 1813. Francis SPAULDING and Nancy Foster, dau. John Foster
who is surety. Married 22 December by Rev. James Robinson. p 494

8 December 1792. Thomas SPAULDING and Martha Parsons, dau. William
Parsons who is surety. Thomas son of John Spaulding. p 178

31 March 1812. Frederick SPEECE, Esq. and Nancy B. Morton, dau. Little
Joe Morton. Married 2 April by Rev. John H. Rice. Sur. John Morton.
p 480

8 September 1772. Henry SPEED and Elizabeth Julia Spencer, dau. Thomas
Spencer. Sur. Sian Spencer. p 14

7 December 1767. James SPEED and Mary Spencer, dau. Thomas Spencer.
Sur. Thomas Speed. p 5

4 December 1810. Charles SPENCER and Polly Puckett, dau. Jacob Puckett.
Sur. Samuel Walker. Married 5 December by Rev. Joshua Worley. p 447

17 September 1786. Gideon SPENCER and Catherine Clements, ward of M.
Clements. Sur. John M. Read. Married 21 September by Rev. Thomas
Johnston. p 86

9 June 1802. Henry SPENCER and Sally Bouldin, dau. James Bouldin who is
surety. Married 10 June by Rev. William Spencer. p 320

28 July 1782. Himais (?) SPENCER and Joyce Franklyn. Married by Rev.
John Weatherford. Ministers' Returns p 2

23 April 1788. John SPENCER and Drucilla Bedford (widow of Thomas
Bedford). Sur. Thomas Read. Married 24 April by Rev. Edward Almond.
p 120

15 June 1810. Joseph SPENCER and Aney Rowton, dau. William Rowton.
Sur. Charles Spencer. p 458

27 November 1786. Robert SPENCER and Lucy Weatherford, dau. Richard
Weatherford who is surety. p 87

13 May 1799. Samuel SPENCER and Agnes Woodson Daniel, dau. John Daniel.
Sur. Stephen Bedford. p 276

26 October 1798. Sharp SPENCER and Polly Marshall, dau. William
Marshall. Sur. Charles McKinney. p 265

10 April 1794. Thomas A. SPENCER and Jemima Overton. Married by Rev.
William Mahon. Ministers' Returns p 17

7 September 1796. Thomas C. SPENCER and Frances Pearce, dau. Martin
Pearce. Sur. Thomas Spencer. Married by Rev. Archibald Alexander
who says Pierce. p 242

22 December 1801. Thomas SPENCER and Polly Spaulding, dau. John Spaulding. Sur. William Parsons. Married 24 December by Rev. Obadiah
Edge. p 306

5 January 1801. William SPENCER and Judith Lowell, dau. Thomas Lowell.
Sur. Charles Spencer. Married same day by Rev. Bernard Todd. p 300

7 January 1793. Thomas SPRAGGINS and Nancy Bumpass. Sur. William Royal.
Married 16 January by Rev. John Williams. p 190

31 October 1803. John STANDISH and Catherine Ward. Sur. John Rawlins,
Jr. Married 25 (?) October by Rev. Edward Almond who says Catherine
Waid. p 344

6 April 1812. Eli STAPLES and Elizabeth D. Williams, dau. Matthew
Williams. Sur. Nelson Watson. Married 30 April by Rev. Richard
Dabbs.

25 March 1788. John STEAGALL and Susanna Portwood. Sur. Lloyd Portwood. p 120

28 January 1794. John STEAGALL and Susannah Portwood. Married by Rev.
Edward Almond. Ministers' Returns p 18

7 December 1801. Thomas Augustine STEPHENSON and Polly Adams, dau.
James Adams who is surety. Married 17 December by Rev. Edward Almond.
p 309

3 January 1791. Peter STERN and Elizabeth Jennings. Sur. Thomas Harvey.
p 155

14 November 1792. Abraham ST. JOHN and Mary Harris, dau. John Haris
who is surety. Married 15 November by Rev. Obadiah Edge. p 181

24 December 1808. Isaac ST. JOHN and Betsey Lawson, dau. James Lawson
who is surety. p 422

31 August 1793. Major ST. JOHN and Sarah Tackett, dau. Francis Tackett.
Sur. John Tackett. Major son of Elizabeth St. John. Married 2
September by Rev. Obadiah Edge. p 191

6 February 1793. William ST. JOHN and Betsey Penticost, dau. William
Penticost. Sur. Richard Penticost. Married 8 February by Rev.
Obadiah Edge. p 190

6 April 1801. Lemuel STOE and Sarah Barnes. Sur. Gabriel Barnes.
Married 16 April by Rev. John Chappell. p 305

19 July 1784. Allen STOKES and Martisha May, dau. Henry May. Sur.
Stephen May. p 61

3 February 1783. David STOKES and Molly Meriwether Marable, dau.
Nathaniel Marable. Sur. Paul Carrington. Married 6 February by Rev.
Thomas Johnston. p 55

26 August 1815. Henry STOKES and Polly Tatum, dau. Garnett Tatum. Sur.
Benjamin Tatum. Henry son of Thomas Stokes. Married 30 August by
Rev. James Robertson. p 526

15 February 1815. James STOKES and Sally Sublett. Married by Rev.
Thomas E. Jeter. Ministers' Returns p 43

8 May 1810. James STOKES and Polly Duffer, dau. Edmund Duffer who is
surety. Married 9 May by Rev. Richard Dabbs. p 446

21 February 1786. Josiah STOKES and Mary Hance, dau. John Hance. Sur. Will Brizendine. Married 23 February by Rev. John Williams who says Mary Haines. p 96

18 February 1786. Jacob STOWE and Nancy Ford. Married by Rev. Thomas Johnston. Ministers' Returns p 6

10 March 1786. Joel STOWE and Frances St. John, dau. Abraham St. John. Sur. Jacob St. John. Married 19 March by Rev. John Weatherford. p 86

29 March 1803. John STOWE and Sarah Middleton, widow of James Middleton. Sur. James Adams. Returned 1 December by Rev. John Chappell. p 340

15 November 1787. William STOWE and Cleary Barnes, dau. Henry and Sarah Barnes. Sur. Gabriel Barnes. Married 21 November by Rev. John Weatherford. p 104

30 August 1810. Stephen STOWELL and Jinsey Hannah. Sur. James Hannah. p 446

26 November 1788. Henry STRANGE and Susanna Nance Sullivant, dau. M Sullivant who is surety. Married 27 November by Rev. John Williams. p 122

22 January 1803. William D. STRINGER and Mary Tenor. Sur. Richard M. Gaines. Married 27 January by Rev. John Chappell who says Mary Fener. p 340

5 May 1788. Christian STROM and Rachel Smith (widow). Sur. Thomas Flournoy. p 122

9 May 1782. Abraham SUBLETT and Sarah Sublett. Married by Rev. John Weatherford. Ministers' Returns p 3

6 September 1790. Abraham SUBLETT and Polly Smith. Sur. John Smith. p 140

29 December 1788. Jordan SUBLETT and Polly Davis, dau. Temple Davis who is surety. Married 1 January 1789 by Rev. Joshua Worley. p 126

4 November 1782. Valentine SUBLETT and Margaret Brent. Sur. Perrin Alday. Married same day by Rev. Thomas Jonston. p 46

28 March 1787. Clement SULLIVANT and Sarah Lawson, dau. George Lawson. Sur. John Harris. p 106

22 February 1790. Jarrell SULLIVANT and Mary Eudaly. Sur. Archibald Campbell. Jarrell son of John Sullivant. Married same day by Rev. Thomas Johnston. p 139

23 July 1792. Joel SULLIVANT and Lucy Brown. Sur. Burwell Brown. Married 28 July 1971 (?) by Rev. Edward Almond. p 182

3 January 1791. Littleberry SULLIVANT and Nanny Tucker. Sur. Eminoah Sullivant. Married 14 January by Rev. John Williams who says Nancy Tucker. p 156

15 August 1801. Thomas SUMPTER and Mary Todd, dau. Bernard Todd. Sur. John Hunter. p 310

29 November 1790. William SUMPTER and Betsey Wheeler, dau. John Wheeler. Sur. Thomas Sumpter. p 139

11 August 1808. John SWEENEY and Nancy Smith, dau. Thomas Smith. Sur. Owen Smith. p 422

14 November 1789. Lewis TACKETT and Sukey Sumpter, dau. Edmund Sumpter. Sur. William Sumpter. Married 20 November by Rev. John Weatherford. p 127

7 July 1783. John TANKERSLY and Anne Johnston (widow). Sur. James White. Married same day by Rev. Thomas Johnston. p 54

14 October 1785. Richard TANKERSLEY and Mary Helton, dau. Andrew Helton. Sur. Joseph Dabbs. Married 23 October by Rev. John Weatherford. p 76

4 June 1810. Oldham TARPLEY and Mary Brown, widow of William Brown. Sur. Thomas Tarpley. p 460

10 March 1801. Thomas TARPLEY and Jean Warren. Sur. Russell Brown. Married 12 March by Rev. Edward Almond. p 300

7 January 1782. William TARPLEY and Betty Almond, Jr., dau. John Almond. Sur. James Tarpley. p 47

16 January 1809. William TARPLEY and Catherine Palmer, dau. Luke Palmer. Sur. William Palmer. Married 17 January by Rev. Mathew Dance. p 430

30 November 1808. Caleb TATE and Eliza P. Timberlake, dau. John Timberlake. Sur. John Leseur. Married 3 December by Rev. John H. Rice. p 420

12 June 1794. Charles TATE and Abigail Jones. Sur. William Jones. p 218

19 July 1792. Edmund TATE and Lucy Barksdale, dau. W. Barksdale. Sur. Philip Goode. p 173

29 January 1801. William TATE and Lucy Sadler, dau. Thomas Sadler who is surety. p 315

25 October 1815. Berry TATUM and Margaret Jones, dau. Cadwallader Jones, Sr. Sur. David Jones. p 528

14 November 1810. Henry TATUM and Rosy Clark, dau. James Clark who is surety. p 448

12 August 1814. Richard TATUM and Elizabeth C. Robertson, dau. John Robertson who is surety. p 518

9 July 1800. James TAYLOR and Elizabeth Parten. Sur. William White. James son of Francis Taylor. p 299

4 January 1773. Richard TAYLOR and Hannah Varnon, dau. Jonathan Varnon. Sur. Benjamin Parrott. p 21

1 November 1802. Dr. James TERMAN and Elizabeth Povall Lewis, dau.
Charles Lewis. Sur. Daniel Williams. p 320

6 November 1783. Joseph TERRELL and Elizabeth Chisolm. Married by
Rev. Thomas Johnston. Ministers' Returns p 4

5 April 1791. Dabney TERRY and Fanny Haily, dau. Thomas Haily who is
surety. p 155

7 December 1796. Charles THARP and Betsey Dupriest, dau. John Dupriest.
Sur. Simon Jackson. Married 9 December by Rev. John Chappell. p 241

19 March 1788. Terry THARP and Susanna Totty, dau. Abner Totty. Sur.
William Tharp. p 126

8 February 1787. Thomas THARP and Sinah Haley, dau. James Haley. Sur.
Robert Roberts. Married by Rev. Thomas Johnston who says 14 July.
p 107

3 March 1800. Job H. THOMAS and Betsey Barnes, dau. James Barnes. Sur.
John Barnes. Job son of Jesse Thomas. Married same day by Rev.
Edward Almond. p 299

6 March 1786. John THOMAS and Eliner Barton (widow). Sur. Thomas
Scott. p 85

7 May 1793. Nathaniel THOMAS and Sarah Price, dau. William and Sarah
Price. Sur. Samuel Price. Returned to October 1793 Court by Rev.
John Chappell. p 195

22 January 1810. George THOMPSON and Nancy Barnes. Sur. Gabriel
Barnes. Married 24 January by Rev. Richard Dabbs. p 458

21 April 1815. Griffin THOMPSON and Patsey Saint John, dau. Jacob Saint
John who is surety. Married 25 April by Rev. John Chappell. p 529

28 June 1814. John THOMPSON and Crochia Johnston, dau. James Johnston
who is surety. p 515

2 June 1789. Oliver THOMPSON and Polly Anderson Norris, dau. John
Norris, Jr. Sur. Robert Watson. Married 5 June by Rev. John
Williams. p 131

27 October 1779. Robert THOMPSON and Sarah Watkins, dau. James Watkins.
Robert son of Drury Thompson. Sur. William Watkins. Wit. on bond
Hillery Moseley and William T. Booker. p 34

7 August 1786. William THOMPSON and Henrietta Williams, dau. John
Williams. Sur. Matthew J. Williams. Married 10 August by Rev.
David Ellington. p 83

7 July 1806. William THOMPSON and Fannie Dunn (widow). Sur. Levi
Blankenship. Married 29 July by Rev. Edward Almond. p 390

15 October 1801. Francis THORNTON and Anne Pettus. Married by Rev.
John Fore. Ministers' Returns p 27

27 May 1812. Francis M. THORNTON and Elizabeth Roach (widow). Sur.
John Thompson. p 479

22 March 1813. Francis W. THORNTON and Polly Clark, dau. Edward Clark
who is surety. Married 23 March by Rev. Thomas E. Jeter. p 493

1 January 1810. Richard THORNTON and Sally Sterling Smith, dau. Robert
Smith. Sur. William L. Thornton. p 460

5 December 1796. William L. THORNTON and Susanna Harvey. Sur. Francis
Thornton. p 241

15 February 1797. Thomas THROCKMORTON and Susanna Morton. Sur. William
Hill. p 262

13 October 1773. John THURSTON and Aley Taylor, dau. James Taylor.
Sur. Henry Kay. p 19

24 December 1785. William THWEAT and Sally Gilliam, dau. James Gilliam.
Sur. James Johnston. Married by Rev. Thomas Johnston who says
27 November. p 76

16 April 1791. Thomas TILLER and Sally Kemp, dau. Francis Kemp. Sur.
John Whitlow. Married 21 April by Rev. Obadiah Edge. p 160

4 February 1793. Thomas TILLER and Tabitha Hunt, widow of Charles Hunt.
Sur. James Johnston. Returned to May 1793 Court by Rev. John
Chappell. p 198

12 February 1779. Thomas TINSLEY and Tabitha Spencer, dau. Ahimas
Spencer. Sur. Thomas Spencer. p 33

- February 1801. Mordicai TOMPKINS and Mary Alday. Married by Rev.
Bernard Todd. Ministers' Returns p 28

14 September 1790. Emanuel TOOMBS and Betsey Gankins, dau. John Ginkins.
Sur. William Roberts. p 142

21 November 1793. Abner TOTTY and Mary White, dau. Sarah Matthews.
Sur. William Totty. p 189

5 December 1791. Archelous (Archibald) TOTTY and Liddy Stow, dau.
Susanna Stow. Sur. James St. John. p 167

3 September 1804. Arthur TOTTY and Nancy Graves, dau. William Graves
who is surety. Married 20 September by Rev. Richard Dabbs, Jr. p 364

23 August 1770. Thomas TOTTY and Mary Mann. Sur. Burwell Vaiden. p 8

6 May 1815. Edward TOWLER and Nancy Friend, dau. Joseph Friend, Sr.
Sur. B. W. Lester. p 528

13 September 1790. John TOWLER and Anna Almond. Sur. James Elmore.
p 148

2 March 1778. Joel TOWNES and Frankey Gaines, dau. Richard Gaines who
is surety. p 29

18 February 1804. John TOWNES and Lucy Cook, dau. Raines Cook. Sur.
Michael Maddox. p 364

6 January 1809. James TRAYLOR and Nancy Cardwell, dau. Peter Cardwell. Sur. Joseph Davis. Married by Rev. Mathew Lyle. p 431

2 January 1783. Reuben TRAYNUM and Judith Overton. Married by the Rev. Thomas Johnston. Ministers' Returns p 1

19 June 1806. Reuben TRAYNUM and Elizabeth Hart (widow). Sur. Reuben Lipscomb. p 390

10 May 1793. William TRAYNUM and Milly Redmon. Sur. Matthews Williams. Married 20 May by Rev. Thomas Dobson. p 197

5 January 1795. Benjamin TRENT and Susanna Copeland, dau. W. Copeland. Sur. Philip Copeland. Married 8 January by Rev. Joshua Worley. p 226

19 December 1801. Eppa TUCKER and Elizabeth Johns, dau. John Johns. Sur. Pascal Tucker. See Eppes Tucker. p 307

24 December 1801. Eppes TUCKER and Elizabeth Johns. Married by Rev. John Chappell. See Eppa Tucker. Ministers' Returns p 27

20 October 1810. Epps TUCKER and Elizabeth Vaughan, dau. Zedekiah Vaughan. Sur. Francis Vaughan. p 459

1 February 1796. Merriman TUCKER and Anna Overstreet, dau. William Overstreet. Married 4 February by Rev. John Chappell. p 242

19 February 1803. Paschal TUCKER and Polly Penticost, dau. William Penticost. Sur. Lewis Y. Beadles. Married 24 February by Rev. John Chappell. p 339

28 March 1782. William TUCKER and Mary Cole. Sur. Daniel Ellington. Married 30 March by Rev. Thomas Johnston. p 50

13 December 1788. Edmund TURNER and Margaret Cage, dau. Benjamin Cage. Sur. Gabriel Barnes. p 126

6 July 1795. George TURNER and Polly Rowlett. Sur. William Rowlett. p 226

28 December 1772. Lewis TYLER and Mary B. Palmer, dau. John Palmer. p 14

3 March 1810. Ebenezer VARNER and Nancy Hitchcock (widow). Sur. John McMichael. Married same day by Rev. John Chappell. p 445

29 August 1797. James VARNER and Nancy McMichael. Married by Rev. John Chappell. See James Vernon. Ministers' Returns p 22

3 September 1790. Joseph VARNER and Molly McKenney. Sur. Morris McKenney. Married 7 October by Rev. Henry Lester. p 151

20 April 1807. Ashley VAUGHAN and Jane Gregory, dau. Joseph Gregory. Sur. Hezekiah McCargo. Married 22 April by Rev. David McCargo. p 406

2 June 1790. Bolling VAUGHAN and Susanna Fuqua. Married by Rev. John Williams. See Bouldin Vaughan. Ministers' Returns p 11

1 June 1790. Bouldin VAUGHAN and Susanna Fuqua, dau. John Fuqua. Sur. John Vaughan. See Bolling Vaughan. p 145

3 October 1806. Francis VAUGHAN and Anna Rice (widow of John Rice). Sur. Thomas Johns. Married same day by Rev. John Chappell. p 392

2 August 1809. Griffin VAUGHAN and Elizabeth Matthews. Sur. William Matthews. Married 3 August by Rev. Joseph Jenkins. p 431

5 October 1789. James VAUGHAN and Sarah Dabbs, dau. Richard Dabbs. Sur. John Foster. Married 15 October by Rev. Thomas Johnston. p 133

28 November 1804. James VAUGHAN and Jincey Clement, dau. Jane Elmore. James son of William Vaughan who is surety. p 352

2 April 1806. James VAUGHAN and Nancy Hatchett, dau. Thomas Hatchett who is surety. Married 3 April by Rev. Richard Dabbs, Jr. p 392

5 October 1792. John VAUGHAN and Nancy Callicot. Sur. Henry Hughes. p 179

9 June 1794. John VAUGHAN and Betty Mullins. Sur. William Mullins. p 218

31 August 1812. Josiah VAUGHAN and Prudence Clark, dau. Elijah Clark. Sur. John Clark. p 479

23 November 1801. Lewis VAUGHAN and Mary Childrey, dau. Benjamin Childrey. Sur. Thomas Childrey. p 311

5 January 1789. Ligon VAUGHAN and Dicea Calicot, dau. Beverley Calicot. Sur. Gabriel Sibley. Married 15 January by Rev. John Williams who says Callicott. p 134

23 September 1781. William VAUGHAN and Patsey Mimms, dau. Thomas Mimms. Sur. James Vaughan. p 44

5 January 1797. Samuel VAUGHTERS and Obedience Jackson. Sur. John Harvey. p 260

11 December 1784. Anthony VEIDEL and Edith Brewer, dau. Sackville Brewer who is surety. See Anthony Verdel. p 66

4 August 1783. Abraham VENABLE and Mary Morton, dau. Samuel Morton. Sur. Bryant Farguson. Married 7 August by Rev. John B. Smith. p 54

- May 1797. Richard N. VENABLE and Polly Morton. Married by Rev. Archibald Alexander. Ministers' Returns p 21

15 December 1786. Robert VENABLE and Sally Madison, dau. Henry Madison. Sur. Thomas Pettus. p 92

28 December 1784. Anthony VERDEL and Edith Brewer. Married by Rev. Thomas Johnston. See Anthony Veidel. Ministers' Returns p 4

21 November 1815. Harrison VERNON and Polly Vernon, dau. Robert Vernon. Sur. James Vernon. p 528

7 August 1797. James VERNON and Nancy McMichael. Sur. Ebenezer Vernon. Married 29 August by Rev. John Chappell. See James Varner. p 262

12 September 1814. Nehemiah VERNON and Elizabeth Claybrook, dau. Josiah Claybrook who is surety. p 514

24 March 1813. William VERNON and Anne Beadles, dau. William Beadles who is surety. Married 25 March by Rev. Richard Dabbs. p 492

15 October 1768. Edward WADE and Letty Martin, dau. Abraham Martin. Sur. Will Wade. p 7

8 August 1787. Elisha WADE and Mary Ann Stowe, dau. Susanna Stowe. Sur. John Huntsman. Married 10 August by Rev. John Weatherford who says Mary Anne Lowe. p 105

28 November 1791. John WAKEFIELD and Levice Clarke, dau. Samuel Clark. Sur. Samuel Wakefield. p 168

14 January 1791. Samuel WAKEFIELD and Elizabeth Scates, dau. William Scates. Sur. George Burrass. p 162

21 March 1799. Abraham WALKER and Salley Bailey, dau. Elizabeth Bailey. Sur. Philip Vaughan. Married 22 March by Rev. John Chappell who says Sally Baley. p 277

20 December 1778. Anthony WALKER and Suckey Bedford, dau. Thomas Bedford. Sur. Thomas Bedford, Jr. Wit. on bond William F. Booker. Susanna in father's will. p 29

26 December 1814. Beverley WALKER and Rebecca Covington, dau. Martin Covington. Sur. George Covington. Beverly Walker of Campbell County and son of Thomas Walker. Married 28 December by Rev. Joshua Worley. p 513

20 November 1810. David WALKER and Mary A. LeGrande, dau. Josiah LeGrande. Sur. Samuel C. LeGrande. Married 28 November by Rev. Richard Dabbs who says Polly. p 462

3 December 1798. Gabriel WALKER and Susannah Wheeler, dau. John Wheeler, Sr. Sur. John Wheeler. p 273

4 December 1800. Jeremiah WALKER and Amy Hankins. Married by Rev. William Spencer. Ministers' Returns p 25

21 December 1813. John WALKER and Susanna McDearman, dau. Thomas McDearman. Sur. Flanders Tyree. Married 22 December by Rev. John Chappell. p 492

16 March 1786. Marady WALKER and Nancy Hundley, dau. Ambrose Hundley. Sur. Charles Walker. Marady son of Joseph Walker. See Merida Walker. p 93

23 April 1786. Merida WALKER and Nancy Hundley. Married by Rev. John Williams. See Marady Walker. Ministers' Returns p 5

4 December 1810. Samuel WALKER and Patsey Hannah. Sur. Charles
Spencer. Married 8 December by Rev. Bernard Todd. p 445

30 October 1811. Thomas P. WALKER and Nancy Moon, dau. Thomas Moon.
Sur. Isham Moon. Thomas P. Walker of Campbell County, son of Thomas
Walker. p 464

6 January 1797. William WALKER and Elizabeth Jones, dau. William Jones
who is surety. p 261

9 February 1801. William H. WALKER and Elizabeth Mann, dau. Ezekiel
Mann who is surety. William son of Thomas Walker. p 310

5 September 1785. John WALLACE and Lucy Irby, dau. Susannah Irby. Sur.
Robert Rakestraw. Married 8 September by Rev. Thomas Johnston. p 79

1 March 1790. John WALLACE and Lydia Chaffin. Sur. Joshua Chaffin.
Married 11 March by Rev. Thomas Johnston who says Letty Chaffin. p 150

3 February 1812. William WALLACE and Prudence Weatherford, dau. Samuel
Weatherford. Sur. Austin Clements. p 478

6 December 1784. Samuel WALTER and Sally Woodall, dau. Sampson Woodall.
Sur. John Woodall. Married 12 October (?) by Rev. John Weatherford.
p 61

7 January 1793. John WALTHALL and Catherine Madison. Sur. Henry
Madison. Returned to May 1793 Court by Rev. John Chappell. p 188

5 June 1775. Joseph WARD and Elizabeth Huntsman, dau. Lawrence Huntsman. Sur. Adam Huntsman. p 26

16 March 1771. William WARD and Anne Francis, dau. Joseph Francis who
is surety. p 11

1 January 1798. Allen WARREN and Jennie Spencer, dau. John Spencer.
Sur. Burwell Brown. p 264

2 April 1787. John WARREN and Elizabeth Fuqua, dau. Joseph Fuqua. Sur.
Joseph Oliver. p 105

2 October 1797. William WARREN and Nancy Roberson. Sur. George Coleman
Martin. p 262

19 August 1795. George WATKINS and Patience Watkins. Sur. William
Watkins, Jr. p 229

20 August 1812. Henry N. WATKINS, Esq. and Mildred S. Edmunds. Sur.
Archibald Vaughan. Married 31 August by Rev. John H. Rice. p 477

10 May 1773. Richard WATKINS and Elizabeth Parish. Richard son of
William Watkins. Sur. Thomas Morton. p 18

19 February 1785. Robert WATKINS and Frances Morton, dau. William
Morton. Sur. Thomas Read. Married 24 February by Rev. John B.
Smith. p 71

14 October 1802. Thomas WATKINS and Betsey A. Le Grand, dau. Joseph Le Grand. Sur. Jacob Morgan. Married same day by Rev. William Spencer. p 322

1 October 1810. William WATKINS and Susan W. Spencer. Sur. John D. Richardson. p 462

1 October 1792. Thomas WATTS and Sally Overton. Sur. Reuben Traynum. Thomas son of Samuel Watts. Married 15 November by Rev. Thomas Dobson. p 173

6 October 1788. Benjamin WEATHERFORD and Nancy Sparks. Sur. John Carrier. Married 12 November by Rev. Edward Almonds. p 125

19 December 1806. Daniel WEATHERFORD and Susanna Haley. Sur. Humphrey Haley. p 382

17 August 1814. Jonas WEATHERFORD and Judith Rawlins, dau. Neff Rawlins. Sur. Littleberry Chaffin. Jonas son of William Weatherford. p 514

19 December 1810. Joseph WEATHERFORD, Jr. and Molly Cully. Sur. Dr. Franklin Fuqua. Married 26 December by Rev. William Richards. p 445

4 March 1805. Samuel WEATHERFORD and Lina Chaffin, dau. Thomas Chaffin who is surety. Married same day by Rev. Edward Almond. p 370

28 October 1812. Samuel WEATHERFORD and Sarah Petty, dau. John and Hannah Petty. Sur. Francis Petty. Married 29 October by Rev. George Petty. p 486

4 May 1782. Stephen WEATHERFORD and Obedience Fuqua. Married by Rev. Thomas Johnston. Ministers' Returns p 1

16 August 1808. William WEATHERFORD, Jr. and Nancy Weatherford, dau. Stephen Weatherford. Sur. Coleman Chaffin. William Jr. son of William Weatherford, Sr. p 419

8 May 1811. William C. WEATHERFORD and Rebecca Hamlett, dau. William Hamlett. Sur. Charles P. Powers. Married 9 May by Rev. Richard Dabbs. p 463

11 December 1797. Lazarus WEBB and Mary S. Foster. Sur. William Foster. p 261

7 September 1807. Lazarus WEBB and Fanny Terry, ward of Lazarus Webb. Sur. Singleton Foster. Married 8 September by Rev. Richard Dabbs, Jr. p 409

3 August 1807. Charles WEBSTER and Elizabeth Newcomb, dau. John Newcomb. Sur. James Bottom. Married 5 August by Rev. George Petty. p409

11 December 1785. Randolph WEBSTER and Elizabeth Ward, dau. Catherine Ward. Sur. Mack Hamblin. Married same day by Rev. John Williams. p 77

5 June 1795. William WEBSTER and Nancy Staples, dau. William Staples. Sur. William Hutchinson. Married 19 June by Rev. Edward Almond. p 229

25 September 1789. William WEEKLEY and Magdalen Burton. Married by Rev. John Weatherford. Ministers' Returns p 11

2 October 1782. Abner WELLS and Martha Flournoy, dau. Matthew Flournoy. Sur. Richard Worsham. Married 29 October by Rev. Thomas Johnston. p 47

23 August 1790. Lewis WEST and Elizabeth Dabney Whitlock. Sur. Charles Whitlock. Married by Rev. John Chappell. p 147

28 January 1789. John WHEELER and Mildred Whitlow. Sur. Henry Whitlow. Married 27 July by Rev. John Weatherford. p 130

1 October 1804. John WHEELER, Sr. and Elener Wood. Sur. Jacob Morton. Married 4 October by Rev. Bernard Todd. p 360

21 April 1801. Samuel WHEELER and Rhoda McKinney, dau. Charles McKinney who is surety. Samuel son of John Wheeler, Sr. Married 23 April by Rev. Joshua Worley. p 308

29 November 1791. William WHEELER and Nancy Hewett, dau. John Hewett. Sur. Warner Hewett. p 166

19 December 1795. John WHITE and Dorothy Holt, dau. Rachel Holt. Sur. Charles Tate. p 228

26 September 1799. John WHITE and Elizabeth Moseley, dau. John Moseley. Sur. John Armistead. John son of William White. Married 1 October by Rev. Obadiah Edge. p 275

16 January 1800. John WHITE and Betsy Dunn. Married by Rev. Edward Almond. Ministers' Returns p 25

30 August 1785. Joseph WHITE and Rebecca Rice, dau. Thomas Rice. Sur. Samuel Rice. Married 31 August by Rev. Thomas Johnston. p 79

15 July 1790. William Williams WHITE and Disee Taylor, dau. John and Frankey Taylor. Sur. James Harvey. Married same day by Rev. Henry Lester who says Elizabeth Taylor. p 153

31 December 1799. Thomas WHITIS (?) and Priscilla Davis. Married by Rev. John Chappell. Ministers' Returns p 24

13 October 1800. Achilles WHITLOCK and Anges W. Barksdale, dau. Claiborne Barksdale. Sur. William Barksdale. Achilles Whitlock of Halifax Co. p 288

3 February 1785. Francis WHITLOW and Elizabeth Bullington, dau. William Bullington. Sur. Darbey Whitlow. See Francis Whitton. p 76

1 December 1783. John WHITLOW and Martha Kemp. Married by Rev. Thomas Johnston. Ministers' Returns p 2

20 January 1785. Francis WHITTON and Elizabeth Ballington. Married by Rev. Thomas Johnston. See Francis Whitlow. Ministers' Returns p 5

22 June 1789. Daniel WILKES and Elizabeth Wilkes, dau. Benjamin Wilkes. Sur. Miner Wilkes. Married 2 July by Rev. Thomas Johnston. p 136

5 March 1792. Jesse WILKES and Ruth Bailey. Sur. David Bailey. p 183

4 November 1793. William WILKES and Elizabeth Foster. Sur. William Foster. William son of Benjamin Wilkes. p 201

25 December 1812. William WILKES and Sally Sims Claybrook, dau. Josiah Claybrook. Sur. Jesse Wilkes. p 478

8 November 1791. Charles WILLIAMS and Susanna Cardwell, dau. Daniel Cardwell. Sur. William W. Cardwell. p 168

30 October 1809. Clement WILLIAMS and Nancy Haley, dau. Benjamin Haley who is surety. Married 4 November by Rev. John Chappell. p 429

- -   1794/5. Daniel WILLIAMS and Mary White. Married by Rev. John Chappell. Returned to February Court 1795. Ministers' Returns p 19

12 February 1786. Elisha WILLIAMS and Rebecca McKinney, dau. Jones McKinney who is surety. Elisha son of Robert Williams. Married 19 February by Rev. Thomas Johnston. p 87

5 May 1801. Elisha WILLIAMS and Catey Haley. Sur. Thomas Tharp. Married 7 May by Rev. Thomas Dobson. p 310

24 December 1803. George WILLIAMS and Mary Brown. Sur. John Rutledge. Married same day by Rev. William Spencer. p 334

6 November 1814. Henry WILLIAMS and Nancy Redmond, ward of Allen Gilliam. Sur. George Redmond. Henry son of Martin Williams. p 514

1 September 1783. Hubbard WILLIAMS and Nancy Jones, dau. John Jones. Sur. John Smith. Married 9 September by Rev. Thomas Johnston. p 53

17 October 1801. Hugh Lambert WILLIAMS and Janey Hailey, dau. James Hailey. Sur. Robert Williams. Married 28 October by Rev. Thomas Dobson. p 308

9 March 1767. John WILLIAMS and Betsey Williamson. Sur. Nathaniel Williams. p 5

29 April 1790. John Crews WILLIAMS and Mason Biggs. Sur. John Biggs. John Crews son of William Williams. Married 2 May by Rev. Edward Almond. p 152

10 December 1793. Martin WILLIAMS and Amy Collings, dau. Mary Collings. Sur. James Mullings. Married 12 December by Rev. John Williams. p 204

2 October 1786. Matthew WILLIAMS and Elizabeth Traynum. Sur. Nathan Lawson. Married same day by Rev. Thomas Johnston. p 86

11 December 1812. Matthew J. WILLIAMS and Elizabeth Scott, dau. Francis Scott. Sur. Thomas Read. p 477

1 April 1771. Robert WILLIAMS and Anne Watson, consent of Matthew Watson. Wit. Anne and Judith Watson. Sur. Paul Carrington. p 11

25 November 1801. William WILLIAMS, Jr. and Patsey High, dau. David High. William son of William Williams, Sr. who is surety. Married 2 December by Rev. Thomas Dobson. p 308

11 October 1806. Charles WILLIAMSON and Elizabeth S. Brown, dau. James Brown. Sur. John White. p 399

7 September 1772. Cuthbert WILLIAMSON and Susanna White. Sur. John White. p 13

7 February 1785. George WILLIAMSON and Fanny Toombs. Married by Rev. John Weatherford. Above date when marriage was returned to Clerk's Office. Ministers' Returns p 3

17 August 1805. Jacob WILLIAMSON and Tishey Osborne. Sur. Randolph Ryan. Married 22 August by Rev. Edward Almond. p 369

7 March 1796. John WILLIAMSON and Mason Lawrence, dau. Sarah Thomas. Sur. Littleberry Lawrence. Married by Rev. Obadiah Edge. p 244

6 January 1800. John WILLIAMSON and Elizabeth Jackson. Sur. William Rosser. Married 8 January by Rev. John Chappell. p 288

1 September 1807. John P. WILLIAMSON and Elizabeth W. Chappell, dau. John Chappell. Sur. Robert Price. John P. son of Mary Wiliamson. p 409

11 April 1808. John W. WILLIAMSON and Lucy Townes (widow). Sur. John Fears. John son of Rowland Williamson. Married 14 April by Rev. Richard Dabbs, Jr. p 419

16 November 1811. Samuel WILLIAMSON and Judith Woodfin, dau. George Woodfin. Sur. Charles V. Brown. p 463

3 August 1814. James WILLS and Nancy Baker, dau. Brooks Baker who is surety. p 515

28 August 1791. James WILMOT and Rachel Blankenship. Married by Rev. John Williams. See James Wilmutt. Ministers' Returns p 14

17 October 1782. George WILMOUTH and Tabby Hamlin. Married by Rev. Thomas Johnston. Ministers' Returns p 2

10 November 1806. George WILMOTH and Elizabeth Robinson. Sur. Joseph Wilmoth. Married 11 November by Rev. James Elmore. p 397

9 January 1809. Thomas WILMOTH and Nancy Traylor. Sur. Thomas Blanks. Married 10 January by Rev. George Petty. p 432

28 August 1791. James WILMUTT and Rachel Blankenship, dau. John Blankenship. Sur. David Robertson. See James Wilmot. p 160

8 June 1795. Nathaniel WILMUTT and Frankey Wilmutt, dau. Joseph Wilmutt. Nathaniel son of Jeremiah Wilmutt. Sur. Stephen Blankenship. Married 11 June by Rev. Edward Almond. p 229

20 October 1803. James WILSON and Martha Hamlett, dau. James Hamlett. Sur. Richard Jeffreys (Double Wedding!). Married same day by Rev. Edward Almond. p 330

28 January 1789. James WIMBISH and Lucy Hunt (?) Street (?). Married by Rev. John Weatherford. Ministers' Returns p 12

3 October 1809. Horatio WINGO and Elizabeth Nance, dau. Hood Nance. Sur. Adam Loving. p 429

11 June 1802. Edmund WINSTON and Dorothea Henry, widow of Patrick Henry. Sur. William Cooper. Married same day by Rev. John Weatherford. p 322

3 June 1795. George WINSTON and Dorothea S. Henry, dau. Patrick Henry, Esq. Sur. James Patterson. p 226

14 September 1808. John WITHINGTON and Betsey Tucker. Sur. Jerry Childray. Married 15 September by Rev. Joseph Jenkins. p 423

20 October 1785. Caldwell WOOD and Nancy Sublett, dau. Abraham Sublett who is surety. Married 24 October by Rev. John Weatherford. p 77

15 November 1798. Carloss WOOD and Glaffery Bailey, dau. Nannie Bailey. Sur. Thomas Bailey. p 273

6 February 1787. Irvin WOOD and Usseley (Ursula) Kearsey, dau. Thomas Kearsey. Sur. David Stokes, Jr. Married 12 February by Rev. John Weatherford. p 105

21 May 1790. Joseph Williamson WOOD and Mary Tackett, dau. Francis Tackett. Sur. Lewis Tackett. Joseph son of Ellen Wood. p 151

12 July 1796. Richard WOOD and Elizabeth Thompson. Sur. John Harris. Married 5 December (?) by Rev. Obadiah Edge; (Probably date of return). p 244

7 August 1809. Thomas L. WOOD and Polly Rowton, dau. William Rowton. Sur. James Phillips. Thomas L. son of Owen L. Wood. p 431

14 February 1815. Thomas WOOD and Elizabeth H. Harvey, dau. Isham Harvey who is surety. Married 22 February by Rev. John Chappell. p 529

21 November 1814. Daniel WOODALL and Gracey Stoner. Sur. William Woodall. Married by Rev. Joshua Worley. p 513

22 December 1790. James WOODALL and Betsey Hankins. Sur. John Hankins. p 148

19 November 1799. Elisha WOODFIN and Sarah G. Pearce, dau. Edwin Pearse. Sur. Martin Pearce. Married 21 November by Rev. Drury Lacy. p 278

18 October 1811. John WOODFIN and Elizabeth M. Smith, dau. Thomas Smith. Sur. Owen Smith. Married 24 October by Rev. John Chappell. p 463

26 March 1803. William WOODFIN and Susanna Maxey, ward of John Irvine. Sur. Edmund Dunn. Married 1 April by Rev. John Weatherford. p 330

3 July 1780. Anderson WOODSON and Anne Locklen, dau. John Locklen who is surety. p 37

6 May 1805. Charles WOODSON and Nancy Jackson, dau. Joel Jackson. Sur. John Robinson. Charles son of Tarlton Woodson, both of Prince Edward County. Married same day by Rev. Thomas Hardie. p 370

7 May 1782. Peter WORD and Frances Elam, dau. William Elam. Sur. Harmon Elam. Married 8 May by Rev. Thomas Johnston. p 50

10 March 1808. Joshua WORLEY and Nancy Garland, dau. Martha Garland. Sur. David Garland. Married 20 March by Rev. Thomas E. Jeter. p 423

4 January 1813. Thomas S. WORLEY and Jane Carwiles, dau. Sally Carwiles. Sur. John Childress. Thomas S. son of Raine Worley. Married 8 January by Rev. Joshua Worley. p 492

1 March 1813. Thomas WORSHAM and Lucy Austin. Sur. Hezekiah Ford. p 506

2 October 1793. William WORSHAM and Betty Nevills, dau. Jane Nevills. Sur. George Nevills. Married 3 October by Rev. Henry Lester who says Letty. p 188

11 January 1781. Thomas WORTHY and Elizabeth Keeling, dau. Leonard Keeling. Sur. Thomas Foster. p 44

9 May 1788. Daniel WORLEY and Rachel Copeling, dau. William Coplin. Sur. Isaac Mitchell. Wit. to consent, Joshua Worley, William Marshall and Revey Worley. Married same day by Rev. Joshua Worley who says Coplin. p 125

15 February 1785. Edward WORSHAM and Hannah Garnett, dau. James Garnett. Sur. James Vest. p 77

5 January 1811. John WRIGHT and Kitty Weatherford, dau. Charles Weatherford. Sur. Benoni Smith. p 464

15 December 1802. Andrew YOUNG and Catherine Fuqua. Sur. William Price, Jr. Married same day by Rev. John Chappell. p 321

29 December 1766. James YOUNG and Anne Anderson. Sur. William Anderson. p 3

15 October 1812. John YOUNG and Sally Scott, dau. Francis Scott. Sur. Joseph Wyatt. p 478

5 January 1796. Ralph YOUNG and Croche Ann Mason. Sur. William Mason. Married 7 January by Rev. William Mahon. p 244

23 February 1794. Thomas YUILLE and Lucy Fletcher, dau. Jane Fletcher. Sur. William Price. p 220

22 November 1796. Nathan ZACHERY and Polly Hughs, dau. John Hughs who is surety. p 245

12 November 1800. Branch ANDERSON - Pheobe Jackson daughter Lewis
Jackson. Surety Lemuel Vaughter. Branch Anderson son of William
Anderson. p 294

17 November 1800. John HEATON - Martha Thomson daughter Mary Thomson.
Surety Richard Wood. p 293

26 September 1800. John IRVING, Jr. - Catherine P. Maxey ward of John
Irving, Sr. Surety Paulett Clark. p 294

18 December 1800. Robert JOHNSON - Lucy Martin. Surety James
Cunningham. Robert Johnson son of Philip Johnson. p 293

1 December 1800. George LIPSCOMB - Polly Morton dau. John Morton.
Surety William Morton. p 295

13 January 1800. John LUNDERMAN - Polly Jackson daughter Thomas
Jackson. Surety John Jackson. p 295

17 February 1800. William MILAM - Millendor Loggins daughter James and
Ann Loggins. Surety John Glazebrook. p 295

30 December 1800. John MORTON - Elizabeth Watkins Morton dau. William
Morton. Surety Thomas Throckmorton. John Morton son of Jacob
Morton. p 296

24 December 1800. Hezekiah McCARGO - Tabitha Herndon daughter Joseph
Herndon. Surety Benjamin Herndon. p 296

31 July 1800. William NEIGHBORS, Jr. - Elizabeth Elam daughter Mary
Elam. William Neighbors, Jr. son of William Neighbors, Sr. who
is surety. p 296

13 January 1800. Scarbrough PENTICOST - Polly Pamplin daughter Henry
and Esther (Rice) Pamplin. Surety Stephen Pankey. p 297

4 March 1800. John RAMSEY - Martha Pugh. Surety Matthew White,
Claibrone Barksdale, R. M. Venable and Creed Taylor. p 298

22 December 1800. Bartlett ROBERTS - Rebecca M. Fears daughter William
Fears who is surety. p 297

1 December 1800. Jeremiah WALKER - Amy Hankins daughter John Hankins.
Surety John Nevill. p 297

GAYLE, (Continued)
  Polly 23
GEORGE,
  Sarah 68
GIBBONS,
  Polly 52
GILL,
  Susanna 66
  Tabitha 65
GILLIAM,
  Amy 62
  Elizabeth 56
  Polly Goode 54
  Sally 83
GIVIN - GIVINS,
  Lydia 50
  Sally 17
GLOVER,
  Susanna 21
GOING,
  Betsey 74
  Sally 9
GOODE,
  America 26
  Anne 54
  Betsey 48
  Lucy 22
  Nancy 63
  Polly 48
  Rebecca 62
  Sally 60, 61
GOODWYN,
  Lucy 43
GORDON,
  Sarah 8
GOUGE,
  Polly 70
GRAVES,
  Nancy 83
  Winifred 55
GREGORY,
  Jane 84
  Mary 25
  Nancy 23
GREEN,
  Amy C. 30
  Anne 27
  Eliza B. 60
  Fanny 2
  Letty 46
  Martha 7
  Polly 2, 3
GREENHILL,
  Martha 52
  Mary Petway 48
GREENWOOD,
  Lucy 43
GRIGG - GRIGGS,
  Catherine 62
  Martha 39
  Mary 69

HAILEY - HAILY,
  Elizabeth 52
  Fanny 82
  Jane 14
  Janey 90
HAINES,
  Janey 43
  Mary 80
HALEY,
  Barbara 67
  Catey 90
  Elizabeth 39
  Jinsey 10
  Judith 34
  Lucy 23
  Mary 23
  Nancy 69, 90
  Sinah 82
  Suckey 8
  Sukey 8
  Susanna 72, 88

HALL,
  Dicey 9
  Elizabeth 9
  Milly 67
  Nancy 50
HAMBLIN,
  Nancy 10
  Polly 74
HAMES,
  Elizabeth (2) 26
  Jinsey 56
  Polly Short 41
  Polly S. 77
HAMLETT,
  Betsey 3, 75
  Martha 92
  Nancy 45
  Obedience 53
  Polly 26, 45
  Rebecca 88
HAMLIN,
  Tabby 91
HAMMONS,
  Lucy 34
HAMPTON,
  Frankey 61
  Judith 15
HANAWAY,
  Susanna 51
HANCE,
  Mary 80
HANCOCK,
  Jenny 10
  Mary 54
  Nancy 15
  Polly W. 32
  Sarah 77
HANES,
  Frances 28
HANEY,
  Elizabeth 28
  Nancy 6
  Susanna 77
HANKINS,
  Amy 86
  Betsy 92
  Phelletia 47
  Sally 28
HANNAH,
  Anne 21
  Isabel 20
  Jennie 20
  Jinsey 80
  Judith 20
  Patsey 87
  Polly 21
HANSON,
  Anne 15
HARBOARD,
  Aggey 60
HARRIS,
  Betsey (2) 38
  Elizabeth 11, 68
  Martha 7
  Mary 79
  Nancy 41
  Polly 16
  Sarah 2
  Tabitha 24
HARRISON,
  Anne 40
  Nancy 4, 53
HARROWAY,
  Betsey 64
  Catherine 39
  Matsey 1
  Sarah 39
  Susanna 39
HART,
  Edy 38
  Elizabeth 84
  Elizabeth Coleman 5
  Martha Haskins 38

HARVEY,
  Betsey 46, 64
  Drucilla 38
  Elizabeth H. 92
  Frankey 63
  Molly 35
  Polly 45
  Polly B. 71
  Sallie B. 70
  Sally 16, 36
  Susanna 77, 83
HASKINS,
  Anne 69
  Lucy 61
  Susanna 27
HATCHETT,
  Betsey Bass 29
  Elizabeth 21
  Harriet 14
  Margaret 10
  Mildred 11
  Nancy 85
  Phoebe 29
HAWKINS,
  Peggy 37, 39
HAYES,
  Mary Ann 64
HAYZE,
  Elizabeth 28
HAZELWOOD,
  Elizabeth 62
  Katey 35
  Nancy 69
  Peggy 15
HEATON,
  Nance 28
HELTON,
  Mary 81
HENDRICK,
  Jinsey 77
  Sarah 26
HENRY,
  Dorothea 92
  Dorothea S. 92
  Martha Catherine 40
  Sarah Butler 13
HENSON,
  Anne 15, 16
HERNDON,
  Ann Ritter 9
  Jane 72
  Jean 72
  Mary Magdalen 33
  Sally 72
  Tabitha 59
HEWETT,
  Nancy 89
HIGH,
  Betsey 4·
  Christian 51
  Mary 50
  Patsey 91
HIGHT,
  Sarah 16
HIGHTOWER,
  Nancy S. 34
HINES,
  Elizabeth 45, 68
  Fanny 40
  Tabitha 64
HITCHCOCK,
  Nancy 84
HOARD,
  Sarah 43
HOGAN,
  Prudence 74
HOLLOWAY,
  Elizabeth 51, 52
  Fanny 61
  Rachel 46
  Salley 45
HOLT,
  Amey 48